Chosen Of The Lord - Broken In Heart

This is a testimony to the love and grace of God that is sufficient to redeem every failure, give us hope beyond our disappointments and heal the greatest hurt in our lives.

By Myra Woodbridge

Copyright © 2008 by Myra Woodbridge

Chosen Of The Lord - Broken In Heart
by Myra Woodbridge

Printed in the United States of America

ISBN 978-1-60647-254-5

All rights reserved solely by the author. The author guarantees all contents are original and do not infringe upon the legal rights of any other person or work. No part of this book may be reproduced in any form without the permission of the author. The views expressed in this book are not necessarily those of the publisher.

Unless otherwise indicated, Bible quotations are taken from The King James Version of the Holy Bible. Copyright © 1994 by Thomas Nelson, Inc.

www.xulonpress.com

To Margaret & Robbie,

Our beloved friends that we cherish so close to our hearts. We are grateful for our friendship and trust our journey will continue together until He comes.

Myra Woodbridge
I Corinthians 13:13

DEDICATION

I dedicate this book to Terry, my husband. Thank you for your loving support to see this book become a reality. I could not have done it without you.

***

In Loving Memory of
my parents, Elwyn and Clara Copeland.

***

All Glory and Honor to the Father, the Son, and the Holy Spirit.

ACKNOWLEDGEMENTS

My husband, Terry, and I want to express our gratitude to our dear friends, Margaret and Robert Sampson, Patti and Carl Heiselman, Vera Ferguson, and Rhonda and Cliff Lee for their love and support through a very low time in our lives. Each of you are a gift from the Lord to us and we are most grateful for you and your prayers. Even when we faltered, you would not let us give up but you let us lean on you until we were strong again, as is reflected in the pages of this book. No one could have better friends. You have encouraged me personally to pursue the calling God has given me and to complete this book no matter the roadblocks. Thank you.

We want to give a special word of thanks to the Kingdom Seekers Bible Class at Mount Paran Church of God in Atlanta, Georgia. Your genuine love for us helped to close the wound in our spirit. You are the best.

I want to especially thank Rosemary Nixon who spent countless hours reviewing my manuscript and offering her expert knowledge and recommendations. More than anything, I am blessed with her friendship. Only the Lord can bless her as she deserves for her kindness. Thank you, Rosemary.

Most of all, I want to thank the Lord for enabling me to see my dream a reality. He has amazed me time and again in my walk with Him and this is no exception. He truly is an awesome God to which I owe my life and devotion.

Myra Woodbridge

FOREWORD

The Lord brings people into our lives and because of them our lives are impacted. I met Myra Woodbridge when she and her husband, Terry, visited our Kingdom Seekers Sunday School class. Immediately our class felt that they were going to be a perfect fit for our group. They had attended Mount Paran Church of God in Atlanta, Georgia for years and sat under the strong teaching of Dr. Paul L. Walker and Dr. M.G. McLuhan before the Lord called them to serve elsewhere. It is during this period that Myra's journey begins and her book is birthed. This is not soap opera drama but real life drama.

Imagine one day out of the blue your friend and Sunday School teacher hands you a manuscript. She asks you to read it and to give her your thoughts. Now you know that she is a wonderful teacher and communicator of God's Word, but never did you suspect her to be an author.

I began to read Myra's powerful and beautifully written book "Chosen of the Lord-Broken in Heart" and my heart felt like it would pound out of my body, the hairs on the back of my neck are at attention, and I have goose bumps all over my arms. She writes from such a personal perspective. She makes you feel every emotion of which she writes.

As she takes you on this unique journey, you will discover true Christian freedom. On this personal journey there is an awareness of the life that God intends for each of us. Myra accomplishes this through the identification of spiritual strongholds and the removal of all obstacles that stand in the way of you enjoying that personal relationship that God wants to have with each of us. Myra's journey is about real people with real problems and her story will capture you.

Miracles do happen. Myra Woodbridge's life is living proof; she goes from near destitute days to heart stopping adventures. God has given her such creative depth and her journey could have only been planned by God.

Rosemary Nixon
Atlanta, Georgia

PREFACE

All vessels have a breaking point when the extremes of heat, cold, mistreatment or heavy pressure become too great for the vessel to realistically handle. It may begin very small and not be noticeable. The break may be skillfully covered; nevertheless, the break is still there. Sometimes, the harm is substantial requiring the vessel to be set aside for a season. With love and care, the vessel is restored to its useful purpose. This process can take much time, patience and the intrinsic knowledge of the vessel by its Designer.

This book is about my own season of brokenness and personal restoration. I walked through it and survived because God is bigger than I ever thought and His Word more powerful than I ever understood. I hope this testimony will speak to any broken area in your life and be the balm that brings hope and renewal to you. You, too, are a chosen vessel in which God's purpose will prevail.

Myra Woodbridge

TABLE OF CONTENTS

Dedication v
Acknowledgements vii
Foreword ix
Preface xi
Chapter One — SOMETHING MORE 15
Chapter Two — THE MYSTERY OF THE WILL OF GOD 23
Chapter Three — REAL LIFE IN THE SPIRIT 29
Chapter Four — IT IS ALL ABOUT TRUST 37
Chapter Five — OPEN, OPEN, OPEN 43
Chapter Six — A FAMILY OF BELIEVERS 47
Chapter Seven — TWO CROPS, TWO HARVESTS 41
Chapter Eight — THE PRESSURE COOKER CALLED STRESS 57
Chapter Nine — A CHANGE IN SEASONS 63
Chapter Ten — SURRENDER 71
Chapter Eleven — WORSHIP IS A DECISION 79
Chapter Twelve — THE FINAL BRIDGE TO MY HEALING 85
Chapter Thirteen — WHEN MORNING CAME 95
Chapter Fourteen — EARTHEN VESSELS 99
Epilogue — REMEMBER 103

Chapter One

SOMETHING MORE

In 2002, my husband, Terry, and I were privileged to attend a Sunday morning service at Brownsville Assembly of God in Pensacola, Florida. Rev. John Kilpatrick was the pastor at that time. We had heard of the revival that had been going on there for years. On this beautiful spring morning, we would experience it firsthand. It was also our twenty-ninth wedding anniversary, which made the day even more special. We were not disappointed in any way. There was a holy reverence that was immediately noticeable when we first entered the church. We knew we were in the awesome and holy Presence of God. Just sensing the Holiness of the Lord kept me in tears for much of the service. It was both a humbling and rewarding experience.

During the service, the Pastor opened the altar for anyone who desired prayer. The church's intercessory prayer team was assembled to pray with people individually. I remained seated while Terry went down for prayer for his ministry. He shared his request with one of the intercessors and he earnestly prayed with Terry. We had no idea how or when God would answer. We never do but we can be assured *He will.*

Terry and I have witnessed the Lord doing precisely that throughout our life together. He has answered many prayers for us. He has proved Himself faithful to His Word and to His own. Let me also mention that the Lord will prove He is in control and not any person or circumstance. Sometimes we lose sight of that but it is a reality at all times. Terry and I were at a place in our lives that we would need to remind ourselves of this truth and wait for the answer to the prayer of agreement that was offered in the church service that Sunday morning. Jesus promised if we ask, we will receive. If we seek, we will find. If we knock, the door will be opened to us. (Matthew 7:7) We knew He would not fail *now* to respond to our heart's cry for something more in our walk with Him.

We only need to read the Scripture to see the many examples of how God answers prayer. The testimonies found in the Word will encourage and build our faith that nothing is impossible with Him (Luke 1:37). Prayer works and His answers are amazing and real. It is God's nature to answer prayer because of His loving kindness and tender mercies (Psalm 86: 15; Psalm 63: 3). He *wants* to help us in our time of need (Psalm 46: 1; Hebrews 4: 14–16). Every prayer is answered; however, not all are answered exactly the way we *asked*. That is a good thing. There will be times that the answer is no, not this way, or not at this time because He wants us to confront other issues first. I am not positive that God "delays" answers, but that He simply has an appointed time for the answer.

When we receive answers to our prayers, it can be astonishing as it was for the believers in Acts 12:5–17. In this passage we read of Peter's imprisonment following the death of James, the brother of John. James did not die an ordinary death. He was the church's first apostle martyred for the sake of the gospel. He and his brother John were called by the Lord to be His disciples soon after His temptation in the wilderness (Matthew 4:21). Early in the Lord's ministry these two brothers were given the name Sons of Thunder by the Lord (Mark 3:17). Perhaps they had boisterous or even explosive personalities but the Lord envisioned them as powerful men for the Kingdom of God and they surely were. James' death was not a result of a horrible sin nor was he incurring the wrath of a Holy God. James had served the Lord faithfully. His life *and* his death were a witness for Christ. He and the other disciples understood that following Christ came at a cost: to deny self and take up their cross and follow Him. When Jesus spoke these words to His disciples in Luke 9:23, He was issuing a holy call of individual responsibility to the Kingdom of God. Every believer is to follow in His footsteps.

Suffering in the early church was a fact not to be ignored or avoided. Persecution for faith in Christ was not an isolated event but a reality church-wide. However, in the twenty-first century church in America, suffering *as a Christian* is not a popular message. After all, God wants us blessed, does He not? In reality, a disciple of Christ will experience the blessings of God *and* endure sufferings while living in a secular society. The Scriptures make it very clear that suffering for Christ is an essential truth of being His disciple. We are warned of persecutions by the Lord Jesus in the Gospels (Matthew 5: 10-12; Luke 6: 22-23). On the night of His betrayal, He warned that the world would hate us and reject us. We are not above our Master (John 15: 19-20). We should consider ourselves *blessed* when we are called upon to suffer unjustly for His Name's sake (I Peter 2: 20-24; I Peter 4: 12–19). The example the Lord had given through His suffering and the word He had spoken surely rang in the hearts of the disciples when Herod began his assault on the church. The persecution of James and his subsequent death, unjust and inhumane as it was, is evidence of how wicked and self absorbed the King was. Herod was willing to take the life of a man of God in order to further his own political career.

When Herod imprisoned Peter everyone understood his life had a death sentence hanging over it. One thing Herod could not control were the prayers of the church. The murder of James served to bring the church body *together* to pray for intervention on Peter's behalf. Prayer was a vital part of the lives of the early Christians and should be for present day Christians.

The Lord wants more for us than a quick-fix, crisis oriented prayer life. If this occurs, God has a way of using, not causing, desperate situations to get His children centered on those things that are truly important. We may veer off course from our priorities but the Lord will allow circumstances that will get our attention, our energy, our time, and our resources back on track and in line with His will. I am positive the early church could testify that praying for Peter's life was the real priority of the day and not their personal obligations or preferences. Their example teaches us about prayer as a priority for our daily lives. We are confronted with many distractions in our fast-paced world. These distractions can take our attention from seeking the Lord and His Word, and fulfilling our God-given purpose. If this should happen, the Lord will give us a "holy nudge" of varying degrees to return to our prayer closet and the reading of His Word.

As we see in Peter's experience, it was in the midst of threatening persecution, that the church became centered on seeking the Lord for Peter's deliverance. These extreme circumstances required something more than a casual prayer. Earnest, diligent prayer was the only answer to see defeat of the plan of Herod to destroy the church's leadership and undermine the work of the Kingdom. This was not a battle to be fought in the flesh with earthly weapons. It was a battle to be won in the Spirit with spiritual weapons. This was an important lesson for the early church because they would encounter more challenges to their faith as the Kingdom of God advanced on the earth. This lesson is just as important for the present day church. Earnest prayer is always our first line of defense.

God responded to their prayers and the answer surprised them! He sent a mighty angel to deliver Peter from prison chains and from several guards. The angel required no earthly assistance to complete his mission. God's power was sufficient to complete the task. The church was shocked when Peter knocked at their door to tell of his supernatural release. It was such a stunning answer to prayer! Even though they believed God would answer their fervent prayer; they never envisioned how and when.

As Terry and I left Brownsville Assembly of God that day, we did so with a fresh touch of His Spirit. We did not make any quick decisions or jump on any spiritual bandwagons. We returned to our home church and continued teaching our Adult Sunday School class and we waited on the Lord. There was a sense in our spirit that the Lord was orchestrating a plan for us but He was keeping it "under wraps". He would make it known to us when it was His time. We could not envision how or when His plan for our ministry would unfold but we believed He would bring *something more* into our lives. Something more was just around the corner.

After the Brownsville experience, within three weeks, the Lord moved us out of our beloved Sunday school class and our church home. We were at a loss as to what to do next. Did Abraham, the father of our faith, feel in any way as we did? Could there have been some level of apprehension when he walked away from the homeland he knew, away from his parents and friends, away from the safety and comfort of home? Whether there was a little anxiety or none at all, Abraham continued walking, moving in step with the Plan of God. No wonder he is called the father of our faith! Regardless of personal circumstances, Abraham's confidence remained in God and in the Promise He made to him. Along with his faith, there must have been a desire within his heart for *something more* than he had previously known. Such a desire will drive a person's faith to find it.

Could it be that Nicodemus who came alone in the dark hours of night to visit Christ simply wanted something more than religious traditions and laws? John 3:1-21 records this meeting between the two of them. Nicodemus is the first one to hear the words, "For God so loved the world that He gave His only begotten Son, that whoever believes in Him should not perish but have everlasting life." (John 3:16 NKJV) There was nothing in all his Jewish training and theological studies that ever gave him such a promise. Nicodemus received a grand and glorious truth that night.

The Gospel of Luke, chapter 8, verses 43 – 48 tells us of a nameless woman who was only identified by her condition. It was going against religious rules for this woman to be in a large gathering of people. She was considered unclean by Jewish Law and anyone who touched her was declared unclean (Leviticus 15:19). She was willing to risk the possibility of religious rebuke and embarrassment before others if she was discovered. She wanted something more: to touch the hem of His garment so that she would be whole. The risk was worth it.

Matthew's Gospel, chapter 15, verses 21 – 28 gives us another example of someone who was willing to step out in faith in order to have something more. This woman is referred to as a "woman of Canaan" – a Gentile - from the region of Tyre and Sidon. Her story concerns more than her ethnic race or place of residence. She desperately wanted something more for her demon possessed daughter. She wanted her child to be delivered, to be totally free of the control of the demon. She seized her opportunity to pursue the Jewish Teacher called Jesus because He also worked miracles. The *only* solution for her daughter was a miracle.

When this woman first approached Christ for His help, He was silent. She was not offended nor did she give up.

The disciples wanted to be rid of her so they urged the Lord to send her away. She ignored their hostility and prejudice and continued to pursue Him. After briefly being in His Presence, she surely realized there was something different about this Jewish Teacher. Her pursuit no longer centered only on her request for His help. She began to worship the One she recognized as Lord! Jesus revealed to her the purpose for which He was sent. He was to give Israel, the recipients of the Old Covenant blessing, the first opportunity to accept the Gospel with its blessings. This Truth did not change her pursuit. She was determined to have something more. That which appeared to be a rejection of her request from the Lord was the turning point in receiving her miracle. She responded with an unmovable faith believing it would only take a small portion of His blessing to deliver her tormented child. Jesus was so moved that He declared her to be a woman of great faith and granted her request. Scripture tells us the woman's daughter was healed that very hour. She experienced *something more*.

These are only a capsule of Biblical examples detailing the longings of people's hearts that were not beyond the Power of God to grant. In each instance, the people were willing to take the necessary steps to see it happen for themselves or their loved ones. When we do our part and trust the Lord to do what *He alone can do*, we are in partnership with Him for a miracle.

We must understand that receiving something more in our lives will come at a price. Our pride, our self sufficiency and our personal feelings must be nailed to the Cross in order to pursue Him in humility, worship and bold faith. In order to experience something beyond what we have, demands we do something beyond what we presently are doing. It depends on how much we want it, and if we want it badly enough, we will make the necessary effort to receive it. This holds true in all of life.

Terry and I desired something more in our experience with God and this compelled us to take that step of faith by leaving the familiar and comfortable place of ministry. This was essential before we could experience the next phase of ministry the Lord had for us. The next phase of ministry would prove to be the most unfamiliar place we would ever walk. Our step of faith was not as grand or bold as Abraham's. It was a major step for *us* because we were leaving people we cherished and a fulfilling teaching and leadership ministry without *knowing* where the next phase of ministry would be. In the months ahead, the Lord had additional steps of faith for us that would be challenging *and* rewarding. Many times while walking this unfamiliar path, He would remind us of the Scripture in Isaiah 55: 8-9 (NIV), "For My thoughts are not your thoughts, nor are your ways My ways, says the Lord. For as the heavens are higher than the earth, so are My ways higher than your ways, and My thoughts than your thoughts." God's ways and thoughts would lead us to the destiny He planned as long as we paid close attention to both. He would also provide the direction we needed once we arrived.

Chapter Two

THE MYSTERY OF THE WILL OF GOD

We were in a spiritual haze after taking that giant step of faith and leaving the known for the unknown. We missed those we left behind and the ministry we enjoyed. We surely missed our comfort zone. We were accustomed to being active in church. When we were no longer involved as usual, it seemed very strange to us. We felt so disconnected. We began to question ourselves if we should return to the familiar shore we had known for so long. Were we misled? Or were we headed in the right direction? Regardless of the questions we had, we had to continue to wait on the Lord.

We visited several churches in search of a sign, a clear indication that the Lord had something there for us. We knew in our hearts He would cause the right door to open for us; however, at this point, we were coming up empty handed. We did not seem to "fit" any where! As the weeks slowly crept by our comfort level was dropping. We were perplexed, disappointed and somewhat confused. Would the Lord lead us through such a bewildering valley? Is it not true that if you are in the will of God that everything will fall automatically in place, smooth as silk with no rough spots?

That is not *Biblical* truth though we may wish it were! In reality things do not always come together quickly or easily even when you are in God's will. God would eventually align circumstances and people in our life for His purpose. However, His plan would include teaching us about walking out His will in such a way we would never forget the secrets learned.

Ephesians 5: 17 speaks to us about *understanding* "what the will of the Lord is." This verse gives us a great hint about the will of God – at times we may find it baffling and we need His help in understanding it. In pursuing God's will we will discover there is a mystery about it. We do not comprehend always why we are where we are. It is wonderful yet it is difficult. It is rewarding yet challenging. One day we are rejoicing, and the next day we are crying in sackcloth and ashes. We are left shaking our heads and wondering how we arrived at such a dilemma in the middle of being in God's will. We need *understanding*. However, God does not reveal everything we want to know about His will for our lives but He does reveal everything we need to know, *when* we need to know it. Walking out His will remains a faith walk *one day at a time* trusting Him though we have many questions. Terry and I found ourselves in God's faith-training camp, slightly more advanced than our previous experiences. He put us through the rigors of spiritual combat to teach us to trust Him in circumstances we had never encountered and to understand facets of His will we did not know. The Lord had quite a teaching list for us. I was hoping we would not have to "repeat" any class while discovering more about faith and the will of God!

The will of God is multidimensional just as life itself. Nothing stays the same on planet Earth. Life has a way of shouting at us when we would prefer it be quiet. Even the most spiritual Christian, who is dedicated to serving God, is confronted with life. Life tags us and it is our turn to face a monumental crisis that is harsh and threatening. We experience the enemy coming in like a flood, but our promise is that the Spirit of the Lord will lift up a standard against him (Isaiah 59: 19b).

There is no anticipating the struggles we will face as we seek to walk in obedience to the Lord. We do understand there will be challenges to our faith. Complex situations do not always get instant answers. Being in the will of God is not a guarantee of easy solutions. However, it is a guarantee of His solutions if we do not interfere and attempt to seize control. In other words, we need to avoid taking the matter into our own hands as Sarah and Abraham did. The world does not need another Ishmael. The solutions God brings can be astounding and worth the wait. I am sure Abraham and Sarah would agree. Sarah even thought it was humorous (Genesis 18: 12) but God made a believer out of her. Even though we lacked understanding of the holding pattern we were in, we had to continue to wait. If we rushed ahead of the Lord, we risked birthing something of the flesh instead of the Spirit.

Waiting on the Lord crucifies our flesh. This is difficult because our flesh wants to rule. As we waited on Him to make His will known to us, we did not always wait on Him "patiently". There were times we were waiting with more fretting than patience, more anguish than peace. Even if our flesh is most uncomfortable during the waiting process, God will not change His schedule. We have the option to wait patiently or in misery.

Fretting robs us of the peace the Lord came to give. It opens the door to fear and anxiety. The enemy of our soul will seize his opportunity in any crises to whisper that we missed God or we would not be faced with such a terrible storm. The taunts of the enemy will be: we have failed God; we have disappointed Him; or He is angry with us and has forsaken us. The enemy lies to us. He works on our emotions *in the moment* to torment our mind, to oppress and to discourage us from continuing on and believing God. If we allow ourselves to listen to him, our emotions take over and we function on such a level. At that point, our carnal mind dominates and we are not led by the Spirit (Romans 8: 5 & 6). Instead, our five senses lead us. We find ourselves living on the Street of Confusion with Doubt right next door waiting to rob our FAITH.

A carnal mind sees how bad things are, how hopeless things look and what a failure we are. Our carnal mind tells us there is no point in trying, and there has to be someone to blame for the mess we are in – someone other than ourselves! Fear, depression, anger, bitterness, resentment, manipulation, hatred and pride are fruit of our carnal mind. If we let them, they will rule our life. The resulting behavior of any of these attitudes will rob our peace and contentment. There will be a spiritual tug-of-war within our mind if we fail to surrender any negative feeling to the Lord. We qualify as being double minded which has no reward (James 1:6-8).

As long as we live by (ruled by) our emotions or our five senses, Satan will attempt to keep us on that level of living. If he gains any ground in our lives, he wants to take over. Ephesians 4: 27 in the NIV tells us, "Do not give the devil a foothold." This means we must not give him any opportunity to take over any area of our lives. Satan's plan is one of complete destruction. In John 10: 10a Christ warned us the thief comes to steal, kill and destroy.

God has a different plan. His plan is for us to rise above the emotional level to a higher level where we are governed by His Spirit and His Word and follow in the footsteps of Christ. All three will be in agreement. The Spirit never leads us beyond the Scripture or any way opposite the life of Christ. As we follow the leading of the Spirit, we will win more battles. With each victory, more fruit of the Spirit will be evident in our lives. Galatians 5: 22 in the NIV tells us,

"But the fruit of the Spirit is love, joy, peace, patience, kindness, goodness, faithfulness, gentleness and self control."

Have you ever wondered why it is called "fruit" of the Spirit? I believe it is because fruit is grown and does not develop fully the first season. As it is cultivated, it develops more and more fruit with each season of growth. This is why we experience pruning from the Husbandman (John 15: 2). This process means there must be things cut off from our lives that will hinder the good fruit from growing. The Husbandman wants to see the nature of the True Vine coming forth in the branches. As this occurs, more fruit of His holy character will be evident in our lives. There will be more of Jesus, less of me. The Husbandman works on the branches throughout our lifetime to accomplish the necessary changes. It is not an overnight delivery.

With spiritual growth we begin to think more in line with how God thinks. He does not look at things on the surface but looks to the heart of the matter and the person (I Samuel 16: 7). When we seek to live by the Spirit, our mind is renewed. We function more and more by our spiritual mind. Does this mean we sit around with heaven on our mind and never impact society? Absolutely not. Heaven is our future. We should look forward to it. Living the life God has given us on this earth is for the here and now. He has made it possible for this life to be one of victory and fulfillment.

This victory would be acutely challenged when I experienced an intense spiritual tug-of-war in my mind when I came face to face with grief and loss. It was a war designed to undermine my faith. There would be many taunts from the enemy hurled at me. I came to realize there were choices I had to make to not only survive but also to win the battle. This battle raged as I walked out the will of God.

Chapter Three

REAL LIFE IN THE SPIRIT

Jesus Christ lived a natural life on this earth *by the Spirit*. In every way, His life is the example for us to follow. As a man, He needed those things that a healthy life requires, such as sleep and food. Yet, even as the Son of God, He had to deal with daily challenges. On every level and in every circumstance, He was never defeated. There was no earthly power or spiritual force sufficient to overcome Him. The Cross is evidence of His strength, not weakness. He endured the suffering to obtain the prize (Hebrews 12:2).

If He was teaching His disciples, healing the oppressed, ministering to the multitudes or being harassed by religious and political leaders, He did it all by the Power of the Spirit. He saw people at their worst and He saw them at their best. Neither one changed how He lived His life.

Let us consider some examples. In Matthew 12:22 the Scripture tells us that the Lord delivered a demon possessed man who was blind and mute. The Pharisees were irate and accusatory. When Jesus confronted them, He sternly rebuked them and called them a "brood of vipers" (verse 34). The first time the Lord told His disciples He would suffer many things from the religious leaders and be killed but raised the third day, Peter sought to convince Him otherwise. Peter did not grasp at that time the eternal purpose and plan of God's Will for Christ and the route He would have to take. On this occasion, Jesus strongly reprimanded Peter (Matthew 16: 21-23). In John's gospel the second chapter, verses 13–17, Jesus went into the temple and zeal consumed Him when He saw the money changers doing business in God's House. He took a whip and ran them out of the temple and overturned the tables.

He felt sadness because Scripture tells us He lamented over Jerusalem's rejection of Him and the eventual destruction of the city (Luke 19: 41-44). He wept at the grave of Lazarus (John 11: 35), and He was in great agony in the Garden of Gethsemane (Luke 22: 44). Yet, His mind was submitted to the Holy Spirit. Surely this is how He was able to continue in His prayer in the Garden: "…nevertheless, not My will, but Your will be done." (Verse 42)

Another aspect of His earthly life was that certain things gave Him joy. When He commissioned the first seventy disciples, He gave them specific instructions. When they returned to Him to report on the ministry, He rejoiced! (Luke 10: 21) On another occasion, He said that there is joy in the presence of angels when a sinner repents (Luke 15: 10). I believe great faith in God pleases Him tremendously (Matthew 15: 28) and unbelief disturbs Him (Matthew 17:17). There were days that the multitudes hung on His every Word and other days people rejected Him (Luke 21: 38; John 6: 60-66). Each day of His Life had its own set of problems as well as victories. He may have been confronted by the devil one day, a Pharisee the next, but none could overcome Him. In the midst of it all, He continued to work miracles for those who believed. All He encountered played a part in the Master Plan for His Life.

We learn from His Life there will be days we want to run everyone off, and other days when we want to embrace them. We will have those who are against us and those who are for us. Our cup will have a mixture of joy and sorrow. Everyone on this side of heaven, including the most devoted and spiritual Christian, will not only experience the blessings of God but will also endure the harshness of life. This does not mean we are out of God's will or lost His favor. The difficulties in our lives are simply a part, not the whole, of the Master Plan God has for our life. We have this promise in Romans 8: 28 (NKJV) "And we know that all things work together for good to those who love God, to those who are the called according to His purpose". We discover the *power* of this promise when we face *"all things"* and not only easy or pleasant things. The follower of Christ has the assurance of His presence and His grace that enables us to stand and not fall as we endure the many circumstances of life. The more we allow the Lord to govern our mind as we walk our life of faith, the greater victory we will see. We will realize a supernatural strength during the discouraging, frustrating or agonizing days.

Jesus is our supreme example of fulfilling the will of God for His Life. The rejection and the challenges He faced were essential parts of His Life. The will of God would not have been complete without them. The Cross proves this. The empty tomb confirms God's faithfulness to those who endure. Through it all, Christ was led by the Spirit in all He did and in all He faced and He brilliantly handled every circumstance. He functioned in perfect harmony with the Spirit and the Word. *This* is real life in the Spirit.

Jesus had the ultimate spiritual mind. A spiritual mind is when the Spirit enables us to know, to understand, to perceive, to discern, and to function in this life accordingly. He imparts knowledge to us. He reveals hidden truths to us. We mature in spiritual perception as we are sensitive to the insight the Spirit is imparting to us and follow His leading. It is a matter of learning to recognize when the Holy Spirit is leading us versus our flesh, the world or the devil (Hebrews

5:14 and Romans 8:5-6). It is my responsibility to give heed to the Holy Spirit's instruction. When I do, I benefit. When I do not, I am left with the consequences.

To be spiritually minded is not a matter of having our head in the clouds or being perched on a secluded mountain. The Lord has placed us in an unbelieving world to live a victorious life by His holy power and by His Word just as Christ did. This makes us His witnesses. He equips us to do the right thing when we face the challenges to our faith; however, it is not always the most comfortable or convenient thing. We may lose friends, colleagues, or position when we do things His way but I believe the losses will be short-term in light of the long term blessing of pleasing the Lord. Unfortunately, some may have confused prosperity as being the hallmark of someone being a child of God. God blesses His children with many tangible rewards in this life. The true evidence of being His child is the good fruit we bear in everyday life with all its ups and downs and especially in a season of hardship. We understand that the eternal rewards God has for us can not be compared to the temporal difficulties in this life.

A couple we know faced the passing of their son due to heart disease. The young man was a Christian with all of life ahead of him. Yet, he was taken from his earthly family. Through the loss of their son, the good fruit that was evident in the parent's lives was such a testimony to everyone. Their faith was not shattered though their grief was severe. Their hope remained in the goodness of God and the truth of His Word. Their joy was not in circumstances but in the Lord, and that joy sustained them and enabled them to cope through each day they lived without their son. Their example of faith continues to be remembered in my heart today, and the good fruit that was produced remains to the glory of God.

One purpose in enduring life's adversities is to bring about the best in those involved. We know parents whose child was born with serious problems. The way they handled this life changing situation has proven to be a testimony to many. It brought out the best in them, their family and friends, and their church. The situation belonged to everyone connected to them as each had a part in caring for the child or in helping the parents. Through the years, there have been many crises they have overcome, and they never gave up on the Lord. He has taken them through. It would have been much easier to have institutionalized him and allow him to simply exist. Instead, he has developed in surprising ways among those who love him. He is also a successful student. Faith, hope and love works every time. This is another example where good fruit was produced in the lives of many, fruit that might not have happened otherwise.

It matters how we view our circumstances as it did for these people I have mentioned. Accurate perception and a hopeful perspective are vital to dealing with life. The spiritual mind will see or discern the storm we are facing from a different perspective than the natural or carnal mind. We are able to recognize the storm for what it is and look beyond the adversity to the greatness of the Lord. The storm may be fierce and threatening, but we continue to trust in the Lord and His Word when our mind is stayed on Him (Isaiah 26:3). When we are safely on shore and everything is peaceful, it is easy to believe God. It is in the time of distress that our faith is put to the test. We must continue to believe, hope and trust that He will not leave us nor will He fail us. He will show up, and when He does, peace and deliverance come.

It may be the fourth watch, at the darkest hour, and it may look as though the storm will take us out; instead, He takes us through. This is the Power of Christ living through us! The Lord promises in Isaiah 43:2 NKJV, "When you pass through the waters, I will be with you; and through the rivers, they shall not overflow you: when you walk through the fire, you shall not be burned; neither shall the flame scorch you." I believe God's idea of us "going through" is our overcoming the waters, the rivers, and the fire because He is with us. Certainly, it is not by avoiding them. If the Lord does not change our situation, remove the conflict or miraculously deliver us from it, He will sustain us through it. With each conflict, we learn more about standing upon His Word and refusing to be moved from our trust in God. As we are trained in these spiritual truths, we begin to realize the absolute superiority of the Word of God over any rough waters, deep rivers, or scorching fires.

Our lives are much the same in that we all walk through rough places. Each place has its own shadows. Terry's and my journey has had its share of struggles, but we must remind ourselves that the Lord's overcoming power is sufficient to take us through. His Life and His Word points us to safe passage even if the enemy tries to obscure it in the dark places of our crossing. The obscurity will not last long because the Light will overcome it. We must focus on the Light, not the shadows.

When we face a crisis, if we will hold firmly to the Lord and His Word, the miracle will come. The miracle comes in God's timing and sometimes in degrees. In other words, we arrive on the other side of the storm at the appointed time set by God, but it may take a while. Timing is everything in the Kingdom of God. His timetable operates in perfect precision and purpose. Ecclesiastes 3:1 says, "To everything there is a season, and a time to every purpose under the heaven." God's sovereignty sets His timetable for fulfillment of His good purpose for our lives. We will avoid frustration by trusting in His supreme wisdom in the way that He sets the timetable.

A higher level of training in real life in the Spirit was about to unfold as Terry and I searched for God's purpose for our lives. It would be a path filled with uncertain waters, overwhelming floods and fierce fires where we would learn to trust in God's wisdom and timing in ways we never expected. There was one important truth for us to keep in mind: Someone was walking with us every step of the way.

Chapter Four

IT IS ALL ABOUT TRUST

Trusting God is the bottom line of everything in our lives. We must trust Him as we walk out His Will. When we do not understand our circumstances, we trust Him. When people fail us, we keep our confidence in Him. We learn to trust in the faithfulness and goodness of God based upon His Word and His Character and nothing external. When the enemy tries to deceive us or bring doubt and fear – and he will - we must resist him and continue to trust God. The Psalmist David wrote in Psalm 56:3 (NIV), "When I am afraid, I will trust in you." This was written at a time when he was greatly concerned for his life because of Saul and the Philistines. Fear may dial our number, but our answer must be to trust in the Lord anyway and never retreat.

The devil's plan is to destroy our faith in God and His Word. That is the goal of his attack. He really does not care if we read the Word; he just does not want us to believe the Word. Our faith hinges on our believing what God has said. If Satan can stop one, he stops the other. If he can succeed in this, then the Kingdom of God would suffer. He will use any means necessary to accomplish this. He plants seeds of unbelief in our lives through circumstances and people who may unwittingly be his instruments. From those seeds, doubt grows and we began to question God's goodness and love for us.

Ephesians 6: 11 instructs us to put on the whole armor of God so that we can stand against the wiles or the schemes of the devil. He has many ways to attack. A strategic tool included in the devil's arsenal is to bombard our mind when we are the most vulnerable – when everything is at its worst. The battle in our thinking requires a daily discipline of "girding the loins of our mind" (I Peter 1: 13a) and thinking on those things that are true, noble, just, pure, lovely and a good report (Philippians 4: 8). This requires us to get control of our thoughts and cast down imaginations (II Corinthians 10: 5a). Imaginations such as: "what if", "if only", "why me", "how long", "where is God", "I am a failure", and "God does not care". The list could go on. All imaginations seek to stand against the Word of God in our mind and prevent the Word from being fruitful in our lives. We have to choose which we will believe – the imagination or the Word.

We do not have to surrender to torment in our mind. We can gain control of our thoughts by claiming the Blood of Jesus, appropriating the armor of God, and relying on the Power of His Spirit and the Word. This can be a difficult struggle in the heat of spiritual battle but it must be fought and it is definitely winnable.

In the heat of our battle it may seem that victory is delayed and the loss heavy. This happens even when we walk in obedience. But if we will endure to the end, we will be saved (Matthew 10: 22b). Our race has to be run with perseverance and with our eyes on Jesus (Hebrews 12: 1-2).

It is important that we keep our perspective that all we experience in this life is temporary. Heaven, our eternal home, is our future gain. It is the "getting there" that is the challenging part. In Acts 14: 22b the Scripture warns us, "… we must through much tribulation enter into the Kingdom of God." In this verse the Greek word for tribulation is defined as pressure, anguish, persecution, to be burdened or to experience a crushing. The same Greek word for tribulation is also used in John 16:33 (NKJV) where Jesus said, "These things I have spoken to you, that in Me you may have peace. In the world you will have tribulation; but be of good cheer; I have overcome the world." There must be the pressing or crushing of olives in order to obtain the rich oil. Without this process, there is no oil, no benefit. Tribulation is our *spiritual* process that may be difficult at the time but brings about a great reward. Tribulation develops in us an overcoming spirit so we will not be a pushover for the enemy of our soul or of life itself. Tribulation gives us the benefit of lessons learned. If a battle is lost on occasion, the lesson we learn from that experience will give us the knowledge to be able to stand against it in the future.

The reward for the person who overcomes is written about several times in the Book of the Revelation. One verse is Revelation 3:21 (NKJV) where Christ promises, "To him who overcomes I will grant to sit with Me on My throne, as I also overcame and sat down with My Father on His throne." Christ did not sit down at the Father's side until the job was done, until He overcame death, hell and the grave. He defeated all principalities and powers and made a public spectacle of them (Colossians 2: 15). He did this for you and me. All that Christ endured for mankind became an accomplished work that secured salvation for all who will believe. Anything that we endure in this life, any crushing through a season of tribulation, will be forgotten when we join Christ on His throne.

We will make it to our destination – Heaven – by His matchless grace alone. Our journey will involve difficulties, pitfalls, sidetracks, conflicts, betrayals, and burdens but we have the promise of His presence and His power to assure us of a safe and determined arrival. There will be things that we have no rational, clear cut answers for and probably never will. Faith is not about understanding everything that happens in our lives. Faith is about trusting God in spite of it all and allowing His grace to work in us. James 4:6a (NKJV) promises an increase of His grace in our lives: "But He gives more grace". The more tribulation we endure, the more of His grace we enjoy. His grace is truly sufficient to sustain us through the tribulation until our miracle comes (II Corinthians 12: 9a). I have experienced this time and again.

The next portion of II Corinthians 12:9 has also become a profound reality to me as the Lord promised Paul: "...for My strength is made perfect in weakness...". Paul understood why the Lord was telling him this. He was facing an onslaught from the enemy that was beyond his strength and knowledge to deal with adequately. His strength was not sufficient. He needed something more. We all have found ourselves in this predicament. All we have and all we are cannot be sufficient to deal with everything that life brings our way. At times like this, our weaknesses are so obvious and so is our great need for God's strength. We discover we are not as "spiritual" as we had hoped.

We readily talk about our victories but we seldom want to discuss our weaknesses. We are so geared to speaking in "positive" terms. Weaknesses? Not me, oh no, I am a child of God! I *know* who I am in Christ, I have the authority of a believer, and I have the Word in my heart! All this is true. However, it does not mean there are no weaknesses *within* us. When we submit them to the Holy Spirit, He can turn them into strengths. This will happen when we are honest before God and acknowledge the areas we need help with instead of attempting to be such *spiritual giants*. Any natural strength I have – physical, mental, emotional, spiritual or financial – may falter under the weightiest of life's circumstances. If I rely on God's supernatural strength, I will not falter for very long because His strength will flow into all my weak areas.

Hebrews 11:34b speaks of people of faith who "...out of weakness were made strong". Let us take note that the verse speaks of people of FAITH who also have weaknesses. Scripture never hides the flaws of people of faith but reveals them as normal people with weaknesses, people who faltered. Can we relate to them? Of course we can because we recognize ourselves in them, if not in specifics then in general terms. Weaknesses are a part of the human condition. This simply means that we *need* HIM. He never intended for us to live this life without Him. Emanuel is not just a pretty name for Jesus but it means something – God with us. Since He is with us, He will help us in our weaknesses and struggles of every day life.

Also, we need to focus on the words "made strong" from Hebrews 11:34b. How can weak, fallible people become strong? The people this verse pertains to were not strong apart from God but were made strong by Him. It happens for us as it did for them: when our faith in God is greater than in our weaknesses. It is not in denying weaknesses exist but in surrendering them to Him.

The heroes of faith listed in Hebrews 11 faced inner struggles the same as you and I. They trusted in the greatness of God to enable them to rise above their weakness to achieve things ordinarily beyond their reach. They may have faced their adversary – be it physical or spiritual – with their knees trembling, but their faith gave them strength to do so and walk away with the victory. Hebrews 11:40 lets us know that they obtained a good testimony through faith. Their weakness was turned to strength because they relied on God and not themselves. Regardless of our weaknesses, if we have faith in God, we have something – rather, Someone – who is with us and remains the indisputable Victor over every foe. We are not sufficient in ourselves but the truth is: we are not supposed to be! Our sufficiency is of God (II Corinthians 3:5).

The testimony of the people of faith in Hebrews 11 proves God's strength was "perfected" in them. It came over time. There is no microwave version for it. "Perfected" means accomplish, finish, complete. It is the same word used in Luke 13:32-33 (NKJV) when the Pharisees came to Christ warning Him that He needed to leave the area because Herod wanted to kill Him. Their motive was insincere, of course. Christ did not fret over the plans of Herod nor did He run away and hide. Christ responded to the Pharisees by saying "Go, tell that fox, 'Behold, I cast out demons and perform cures today and tomorrow, and the third day I shall be perfected.' Nevertheless, I must journey today, tomorrow, and the day following; for it can not be that a prophet should perish outside of Jerusalem." His life and death were not in the hands of Herod or the Pharisees or any other person. There would be no premature ending of His life nor would it be by any other means other than the Cross. His life, death and resurrection would be accomplished or completed according to the Sovereign Plan of God. That plan required time to come to perfection, and it would not be thwarted by His enemies.

In time, our weakness becomes our strength when we surrender all to Him and allow the perfection process to be accomplished in us. As this happens, we understand in a greater way than ever before our great need for Him. This understanding became stronger to me as I faced the complexities of walking out the will of God. Jumping through spiritual hoops would not secure my victory. I simply needed to *trust* in God to do the work in me and for me and be confident that the victory Christ won on the cross was for *all* my weaknesses.

Chapter Five

OPEN, OPEN, OPEN

Things were not shaping up as we anticipated in our search for something more in our walk with God. His will seemed hidden. Were we moving in the right direction or the wrong one? We were unsure about the next step in our journey. We were in a spiritual holding pattern. This is not the most comfortable position to be in especially when you have believed it will work out otherwise. We routinely questioned ourselves if we had done the right thing in leaving our familiar place only to find ourselves in the wilderness called *"WHAT NEXT?"*

We shared with close friends our longing to experience more of the Lord and to be used of Him in a greater way in these last days. Also we shared how disappointed we were that nothing had happened since taking our giant step of faith of leaving the known for the unknown. Perhaps we were hoping the earth would rumble or a lightning bolt would strike in the place God would have us to be. We wanted something very obvious to confirm we were on target with the Lord's will. When that did not happen, we determined to set aside a time to seek Him fervently and wait on Him. A hasty decision could mean a wrong decision. We had to have the mind of Christ. Soon we began to have a series of prayer meetings in our home on Monday nights for the sole purpose of seeking the Lord for His will.

The meetings were never for casual conversation or current events. Nor were we trying to convince God to cooperate with our plan and do things our way. Week after week, we spent hours in worship and prayer. We waited on Him for His answer. The Lord did not disappoint us. We had a mighty visitation of His Spirit in these meetings. Every time we gathered together He met with us and He manifested His glory in a magnificent way.

It was during these meetings that the Lord gave a vision to Terry of having a church where there is pure worship and fresh praise. These were not ordinary terms to us. They were concepts that we had not considered before particularly as He presented them to us. Terry envisioned a church where we would not go through the mechanics of worship according to a time clock or religious ritual, but a church where we entered into worship that was all about Him. We do not need a "short order" service. Church is not a café where we place a quick order, eat the meal and get back on the road as soon as possible. It should be a time of sincere worship unto the King of Kings and Lord of Lords. Worship where we actually tarry in His presence and bask in His glory. Such worship is not concerned with who is singing, praying, preaching, teaching, playing an instrument, raising their hands, not raising their hands, being used in one of the Gifts of the Spirit or anything external. It is a worship that is from our spirit to Him in adoration and joy and not contaminated with carnal attitudes.

The Body of Christ must be cautious that we do not worship our worship. It must remain about Him, toward Him, and for Him. It can not be about style. We do not worship a style. We worship God and this was our aim.

Fresh praise simply means we need to give Him glory and honor for all He is in the here and now. How I praised the Lord *last* week is not sufficient for *this* day. I need to give him fresh praise every day that I have breath and certainly in a worship service. We can always find something to be grateful to the Lord for regardless of any conflict going on in our lives. A thankful heart has much more joy than a complaining one.

Sometimes we can confuse church being about us, what we want, what we prefer. I believe the Lord would manifest His Presence and Glory among His people in a greater dimension if we would forget about ourselves and simply make church about Him and for Him – and worship Him.

We longed for a church that was full of the power and glory of God as the first church in the Book of Acts. We believe the Lord is able to do the same today as He did in the first church because He changes not (Malachi 3:6). The first church was all about Jesus, not personalities, not buildings, not superstars, not "my" ministry or "your" ministry. It is not "my" anything; it is about the Kingdom of God advancing on the earth today.

An example of ministry exalting the Lord and not a person is found in Acts 3. The Scripture records Peter and John going to the temple at the hour of prayer. At this precise time a lame man was asking alms at the Gate Beautiful, attempting to get help in the only way he had available. Peter and John saw the beggar and stopped. Naturally, the beggar thought he would receive something monetarily from them. Peter's response was "Silver and gold I do not have, but what I do have I give you: In the Name of Jesus Christ of Nazareth, rise up and walk."(Verse 6 NKJV) The man was miraculously healed! He received something far better than a few coins. His life was changed when the two disciples were willing to stop. They did not hurry on with their agenda to get to their next meeting. After the man was healed the crowd was amazed because they knew him and his lifelong condition. Peter made no claim to fame before these people.

He did not begin promoting "his" ministry, "his" itinerary, "his" successes – not even "his" CD gift offer! Instead, Peter pointed them to Christ and to the cross and to faith in Him. The Lord gave Peter an open door with these curious onlookers. He seized his opportunity to lift up the Lord Jesus and not himself. The church should be about pointing people to Christ and away from themselves.

The first church was about the Lord Jesus, the finished work of Calvary and His victory over death, hell and the grave through the Resurrection. The church has a simple truth: Jesus saves, redeems, reconciles, delivers, fills with His Spirit, sanctifies, makes whole, empowers for service and calls us to bear our own cross in humility. It is a simple gospel, uncomplicated. It is not simplistic, but it is powerful. If we holdfast to this truth and preach it and live it by the power of His Spirit, the present church will be as the first church.

Terry and I sought the Lord and waited on Him to lead us in the search for such a church. Months later, we were led to begin having church services in our home on Sunday mornings. We trusted the Lord to bring the people to the services who He wanted to be a part of this new work. It would be people who wanted something more. Slowly but surely, we were seeing the Lord open this new door of ministry. We were thrilled to be on the brink of a new opportunity to serve the Lord and advance His Kingdom. Only He knew everything that was beyond the door. Thank God, we did not.

Chapter Six

A FAMILY OF BELIEVERS

Time and time again, the Lord amazed us with those He chose to bring into our church family. Each person He sent was especially gifted in ways that were ideal for this church. We rejoiced as we witnessed the Lord building this body of believers to do the work of the Kingdom. We became a close-knit, spiritual family. We valued each other and walked in love toward one another and toward the lost. In John 13: 35 (NKJV) Jesus said, "By this all will know that you are my disciples, if you have love for one another." When we walk in love, there is obvious fruit, and the Lord is glorified. People know we are truly His by this one thing. If there is any claim to fame, this must be it!

When there were crises or challenges within this church family, we would come together and earnestly pray for one another. The Lord never failed to answer. There are people alive today because the Lord answered the prayers from this church family. The Lord intervened for people with cancer, a brain tumor, emphysema, fluid on the brain, throat tumors, demonic oppression, life threatening automobile accidents, and much more. We witnessed a demonstration of the Lord's Power in our services that we will always remember. The

Lord was truly in our midst, and we can never praise Him enough.

Things moved quickly for this new work of faith. We met in our home for a little over three months and then moved into a new shopping center space. In seven months we were ready to move into a church facility. In retrospect, Terry and I cannot say with certainty that the *Lord* was ready. We longed to be in our own building and perhaps that desire moved us prematurely before we were prepared in other important ways. The Lord remained faithful and good to us. He allowed us to make this move, and He continued to work in our behalf as we did. This is further evidence of His great mercy and love toward His own. The Lord never removed us from His potter's wheel, nor will He. He continued to work with us. With this being our first pastorate, there was so much for us to learn and learn we would. He would teach us the value of moving in His timing and much more. He would remind us, time and again, that people are people. Oftentimes, we expect ourselves and others to be more and we are always disappointed. It is inevitable because we all suffer from the same condition: being a fallible human being. Perfection, after all, is found in the Lord Jesus Christ alone.

Once the decision was made to move into the church property, the congregation began working on the changes needed to the interior of the building and the church grounds. God provided for us to accomplish our goal. Many gave time and talent to see the building become a beautiful house of worship and the church grounds enhanced. It was a joy to walk in and sense the peace and presence of the Lord in His sanctuary.

We were basking in the blessings of the Lord. If only we could have bottled this season to keep with us forever! However, a season is not meant to be bottled for keeping long-term nor is anything in life. Instead, each season is to blend with the next, taking away from one and adding to another. Regardless of the nature of the season we walk through, the Lord is not hindered from bringing enrichment to our lives from any of them.

As we worked to see the church move forward, we did not foresee the drastic change approaching our special season. Deep within our hearts our confidence has always been that the Lord will ultimately cause even the worst of seasons to be for our benefit. After things changed for us, that day seemed elusive for a very long time. Nevertheless, we had to hold on to this truth. It would be the most baffling experience we had ever known, a season of loss and brokenness.

Chapter Seven

TWO CROPS, TWO HARVESTS

Opposition happens. We can do our very best to please God but we will still be confronted with opposition. Typically it will come from those we least expect. That is why it will hurt us the most. The Lord faced opposition from the time of His Birth until He was nailed to the cross. Jesus warned that we will face opposition in this life (Matthew 5: 10) and the early church certainly did. Opposition became the prodding stick that moved them out of their comfort zone to fulfill the Great Commission (Acts 8:1). They had been in Jerusalem far too long. If it took opposition to cause the church to move out to advance the Kingdom, then opposition it would be. The Lord wanted them to understand the fulfillment of the commission He had given to them was more important than personal comfort. It was literally a matter of life and death. This remains true today. If we know His will but lag behind in obeying it, the Lord will permit our nest to be disturbed, just enough, to cause us to press into His will for our lives.

Paul the Apostle is a wonderful example of a Christian successfully facing opposition. He certainly had his share.

In the Book of Acts, Luke, the physician, writes about many of the supernatural experiences Paul had while on his missionary journeys. None came to pass without opposition. In the 14th chapter we can read of such an instance. While Paul was in Lystra, a man who had been crippled since birth was healed. The people of that town misinterpreted the miraculous power at work and declared Paul was responsible. They praised him and Barnabas as two of their gods. Paul and Barnabas strongly refused such acknowledgement and gave glory to the Lord for the miracle. In the meantime, jealousy provoked the Jews from Antioch and Iconium to travel to Lystra for the purpose of turning people *against* Paul. Their plan worked. Lystra no longer welcomed Paul. The celebration was over. They only wanted to be rid of him by any means necessary. They stoned him, threw him out of town, and left him on the ground for dead! After they brutally attacked him, there was no remorse. They simply walked away unconcerned for his wounds. Just as important – they were unconcerned that they had caused them.

    This happens in the Body of Christ over and over again. We wound one another and walk away unconcerned. We spiritualize reasons for what we do but it comes down to our own selfishness and our failure to walk in love. "Love worketh no ill (harm) to his neighbor" (Romans 13:10a). Yet, we are harming one another and we are using spiritual terms to do it. If someone says "the Lord led me", or something similar, then he or she *sounds* spiritual enough therefore no one should question their actions. This *spiritual* person sees no need to further explain. There seems to be little accountability. They consider themselves off the hook. Could it be they are misled as those in Acts 14 who sought to eliminate Paul? The people in the Scripture believed they were doing the appropriate thing with every stone they cast. However, when is harming others *appropriate*? There are many wounded soldiers in the Lord's army, often harmed by those within our own ranks.

Opposition may rear its ugly head at the same time we are seeing a great victory as it did for Paul and Barnabas. It can come our way from many angles in different forms. Regardless of the nature of the opposition, every believer is subject to experience a time when we are unjustly treated, thrown to the ground with our face in the dirt, beaten, wounded and left to die as Paul. Typically, the ones responsible will not look back.

The potential for harm comes about if we listen to the wrong spirit and not the correct One. The Holy Spirit leads us in truth and He will always lead us according to the law of love. Love will do the right thing not the cruel thing. If we fail to walk in love, we fail in the most important aspect of being a disciple of the Lord. When Christians do not walk in love, we are no different than the world around us. The line that separates us is not even gray; it has disappeared. Love must define us above our gifts, our talents or our ministry successes. Love never fails (I Corinthians 13:8a).

When we do not walk in love, the flesh is in control. Galatians 5: 19 – 21 (NKJV) tells us: "Now the works of the flesh are evident, which are: adultery, fornication, uncleanness, lewdness, idolatry, sorcery, hatred, contentions, jealousies, outbursts of wrath, selfish ambitions, dissensions, heresies, envy, murders, drunkenness, revelries, and the like; of which I tell you beforehand, just as I also told you in time past, that those who practice such things will not inherit the Kingdom of God." It is easy to understand from this passage when we allow the flesh be in control, we will see devastation. Galatians 6: 8 (NKJV) says, "For he who sows to his flesh will of the flesh reap corruption, but he who sows to the Spirit will of the Spirit reap everlasting life." These are two different crops with two different harvests. It is our choice which one we sow. We all have seen crops sown by the flesh that caused injury, wounds, and destruction. When we are being led by our own carnality, we are more likely to find fault with those we once admired and appreciated. We can become suspicious and think evil toward those we used to think well of, just as it happened in Acts 14 with Paul. These attitudes become the stones we hurl at each other.

Paul was rescued from this plot to destroy him when God raised him from the point of death. In Acts 14: 20, Paul did something amazing: "he rose up". He did not lie in the dirt and nurse his wounds. Paul did not cry over the rejection of the people, nor did he moan over those who left him. He did not become fearful of the possibility of future attacks. He never sought revenge; instead, Paul rose up! He did not give up on God or his calling. He did not denounce the church or any person. There was no blame-game. Without fanfare Paul returned to the city and prepared to leave the next day with Barnabas for ministry in Derbe. He stayed on course with God's purpose for his life. He did not get hung up on people *or* himself. Paul's example has taught me to pray that I not allow the actions of others to get me off course of my purpose and mission from God. It is also my prayer I will not get hung up on *myself* or any person by allowing emotions to determine my responses. Before I *learned* to pray this, I found myself in a place wounded by people for whom I cared deeply. **God** would have to lift me out of my mess and pour healing into my life. Divine rescue came just in time.

In Acts chapter 6, we read of Stephen, who was full of faith and power, and how God used him in a mighty way. How could it happen that a man so used of the Lord became the church's first martyr? It all began with words. Opposition came through the religious leaders who persuaded others to lie and to accuse Stephen of things he did not say or do (Verses 8-14). The *murder* of Stephen began with words! These were the first stones thrown at him. Only his physical death took place outside the city (Acts 7: 58). Stephen proved he was full of the Holy Spirit when he could pray as he was dying; "Lord, do not hold this sin against them" (Acts 7: 60 NIV). In like manner, Paul suffered at the hands of religious people when jealousy provoked the Jews and then their venom spread to others. If only we could lay all our stones down and love one another. How powerful the Body of Christ would be on this earth!

Chapter Eight

THE PRESSURE COOKER CALLED *STRESS*

Stress is a dangerous thing in our world. It is as perilous to our health and well being as any plague. It will affect us in countless ways if we do not deal with it appropriately. Stress will beat us down and dare us to get up. I came to understand its cruelty. In early 2005 the church ministry became more challenging and perplexing to us than we ever anticipated. Our eyes truly were opened to some of the pressures that pastors face every day.

Previously, our leadership was appreciated; however, slowly that view appeared to waver in the minds of some. It seemed that any decision Terry or I made was wrong or at least borderline. Things we said or did were misinterpreted. There were pressures from every direction and our actions were scrutinized. The unity, which we as a church family had enjoyed, was coming unraveled, and it was obvious who the culprit was. The spiritual foe to Christian unity was at work.

The stress was overwhelming, and things worsened personally for me when the pressures took over my life and demanded attention. This did not happen all at once but gradually layers of pressure were woven into the fabric of my life. If the enemy cannot stop us one way, he will attempt to use another tool. The trap had been set.

Stress is so manipulative. Just when you think you have released all your cares to the Lord, stress steps back in to dominate. It incites us to *do* something, anything, to have relief instead of waiting on the Lord. We called on the Lord to intervene in every circumstance. Much later I realized I was only temporarily releasing to the Lord the cares and demands pressing so heavy on my shoulders. I would take on those same burdens again eventually. The Lord obviously needed my help! I would not say that but my behavior did. Apparently, I had the gift of "interference". If the Lord did not resolve things as I anticipated, or in the time frame I wanted, then obviously I was needed to step in and lend Him a hand.

The cycle of church pressures continued. After one problem was resolved another came to the forefront. What a surprise! This is typical church life because church is not a society of perfect people, only redeemed ones that God is still processing into mature ones. A church community is not always free of conflicts but it should provide an atmosphere of resolution. Oftentimes, this is easier said than done, and the conflict escalates instead of being resolved. This causes wear and tear on the lives of those involved.

The stress of dealing with all the challenges caused a great deal of frustration and anxiety, which I kept within. At the time, I did not realize the harm I was causing myself. I only *thought* I was "handling" things when in reality, they were "handling" me. I did not recognize how serious this was affecting my health. For a long time I dismissed the warning signs because I was determined to keep going. This is not a good plan. Eventually, I realized the mistake but only after my health forced me to do so. I was on overload which is never wise. I discovered that stress does not operate according to wisdom. Stress is a pusher, a panic button, a deceiver and it seeks to force its own agenda down our throats. On the other hand, peace and wisdom walk hand in hand with no need to rush but with a calm expectancy that the Lord is in control and will make a way. The good fruit of this union is always obvious in the sweet peace that fills our lives. The fruit that stress bears is always destructive.

Stress knows no boundaries. It invaded my prayer life which is such a cunning attack of the enemy. Too many times I prayed in distress and anguish which only fueled my inner turmoil. I could not understand why God did not change all these circumstances because I knew I was asking Him enough. This perhaps was an indication of at least one of my problems. I was busy telling God about everything and everyone but I was not *listening* closely for His response. My frustration level was off the meter. Yes, I was praying "about" circumstances of great concern and holding on to them at the same time. I was holding on to a time bomb.

There were weeks that I went to the church nearly every day to pray concerning the matters confronting us. One morning as I sat in the sanctuary and prayed the Lord's voice broke through all the disappointment and frustration. He spoke to my heart, "There is light at the end of the tunnel". I thought this was an unusual word for the Lord to give me. I reached for my Bible and it opened to Psalm 112 and my eyes fell on verse 4 (NKJV): "Unto the upright there arises LIGHT in the darkness..." Several weeks later, this word was confirmed to me. I received an email from our missionary friends in Bulgaria, Drs. Tim and Betty Cornett. Near the end of the email she wrote, "There is light at the end of the tunnel". How kind the Lord is to have one of His servants in another part of the world send me confirmation of His word. I have to admit that there were times I wondered how long this tunnel was! I also never envisioned *how* the light would shine through.

In the meantime, my approach to seeing victory would be to pray and fast, declare the Word, claim victory, and the changes *I* wanted would come. This is good theology, correct? Is it true that all I have to do is go through all these spiritual exercises and God will make the changes happen? Sometimes our frustration leads us to a treadmill of works – it's all about what I am *doing* to change things – instead of simply trusting Him. The Lord wanted to help me and He wanted to bring about change for us. He also wanted me to trust Him to do it. Sometimes we are geared for action when He actually wants us to get out of His way and allow our heart to idle until He directs us to move again.

There is nothing we can do in prayer or otherwise that will override the absolute sovereignty of God. Regardless of all the valid things we can do as we seek Him, we cannot force God to see things our way if they are contrary to His purpose. Prayer is not a tool to move Him according to our plans. We cannot expect Him to move against what His wisdom determines is best for us. His wisdom does not always see things "our way". What a shocker! The Lord was continuing to teach me that His way remains higher than mine (Isaiah 55:8-9). It is right to pray and fast, it is right to declare the Word, but the bottom line of prayer is to make our requests known to the Lord. Then we simply trust Him to work as only He can at His appointed time. The results really are His department.

I eventually understood that I had taken on a burden that was not mine to bear but not until my health forced me to understand. We are to bear our cross and not the burdens He never gave us. One of the major burdens we take on is relying too much on ourselves to work things out and not resting in the Lord to do it. Resting in the Lord? I was too busy helping Him. Not only was I relying too much on *myself,* but I was relying too much on *people* to be the answer. Things had become out of balance in my life and God had to open my eyes. The Lord and His word are the only sure answers any of us have in this life. When we get sidetracked into thinking otherwise, He allows us to see the futility of that thinking so that we will trust Him only.

Chapter Nine

A CHANGE IN SEASONS

Change is one of the most difficult things we must face. Usually we want it for others but not for ourselves! However, change is inevitable for us and it impacts the broad spectrum of our lives. Church is certainly no exception and change came knocking abruptly at the door in 2005.

By midyear people who were connected closely to the church and to our lives, decided to walk away. From the beginning, they had been a part of the vision and suddenly they were gone. Terry and I had many unanswered questions. We had been very close and that closeness was shattered. It was a devastating blow to us. There was too much happening around us that we did not understand and none of which could be resolved in our minds. The glorious season that the church had enjoyed was on the brink of facing a monumental change, and it would never be the same nor would we.

Terry and I felt a great loss after the people left. There had been a bond between us that developed in serving the Lord closely together. It was a bond we thought could not be broken. The three fold cord we thought existed between us was in reality more tenuous than strong. One day we were being embraced and the next day we were rejected. It was all too baffling.

Of course their leaving affected those who remained. Everyone was saddened and disillusioned. It seemed as if we were waiting for the next "bad news" to happen. The heart of our church family was broken and we could not piece it together.

We understand that it is not unusual for people to leave a church. It happens very frequently and with ease. Our experience is not unique. Church can be like a swinging door for some. They come in and go out without ever planting themselves. They never make any commitment and there is no accountability. While they have their freedom to come and go, they miss the whole meaning of church and being a real part of a church community where a person's gifts and talents can be used. However, the ones who left were not mere spectators in the church. They were integral components to the church ministry and we loved them as family.

The ones who chose to leave the church in no way intended to cause any pain to anyone. People's *intentions* did not wound us, but their actions. This has been an eye opening experience for Terry and me. We came to realize, in a greater way than ever before, how *actions* speak so loudly and how they can deeply impact people's lives in very real and detrimental ways. Too often we do not consider the consequences of our actions or our words until we are forced to face the results in someone's life. We do not consider those who left the church as our *enemies*. Christians have a common enemy and it is not each other. It is the devil, our spiritual foe, who seeks to make our battle with each other and we start pulling against each other instead of pulling together.

For several months, the spiritual warfare we encountered was unlike anything we had ever seen. Did we open the door to this? Were there people praying against us? Where did the resistance originate? And especially, where was our deliverance? We have faced spiritual conflict through the years. However, this time we were in an unfamiliar battle with a level of intensity that we had never experienced. In the past, all the battles we had faced were only skirmishes in comparison to this one. It seemed like a battalion of evil forces had assaulted us.

I did not know what a broken heart was until this happened in our lives. Grief was overwhelming at times and it seemed as if all I could see were losses. I was getting sicker in my body and in my spirit which put me in a more vulnerable position. It became obvious that in order to regain my health I would need to step away from ministry. We had to be realistic and deal with the circumstances as they were, not the way we wished they were. We had to recognize the season for what it was. God had allowed the season's change to come, and we could not force it to be otherwise. We needed the Lord to show us how to move on.

The greatest sorrow for Terry and me was the overwhelming sense of failure that our vision would not be realized and the humiliation that comes with it. The devil used the disappointment and the hurt we felt to beat us down lower than we had ever been and to devalue us as servants of the Lord. He sought to make us feel that we did not measure up to people's expectations. The rejection we felt was on a scale that we had never experienced. The worst agony in our heart was feeling the Lord had rejected our ministry and that He was through with us. This must be true since a few *people* had rejected us and walked out of our lives! The Lord must feel the same way!

Circumstances were telling us we had failed God. I cannot convey the sadness that was in our hearts at such a thought. Every indication was saying over thirty years of ministry was going down the drain. Our self confidence took a nose dive. We wondered if our ministry even mattered to the Lord because there were many other ministries that were going full steam ahead. The problem really had to be with us! There was such a spirit of condemnation that came against us. It hounded us.

I was walking through a real crisis of faith. I had stood on the Word of God and diligently sought Him; yet, things were falling apart. How could this be happening! Every truth I had held to through my life was being challenged. There were nights I cried myself to sleep to only wake and begin crying again. Sorrow would envelope me. Over and over I would rehearse conversations and actions in my mind trying to determine what I did that was so awful. Each time I would conclude that everything was *my* fault. No one can carry such a burden indefinitely. Even though I had given my all and done the best of my ability, it was not enough. How did we arrive at this point? How could the vision die? It was all so bewildering.

Retaliation was knocking at my door, seeking to gain control. I understood the source of that temptation and I needed the Lord's strength to resist. At just the right time, His message came through to me. I had contemplated calling people from the church to "unload" my burden of hurt and disappointment. I had a truckload. I wanted them to know Terry's and my position; they should know how devastated we were. The Lord stepped in to change my plans. He spoke to my heart that if I would hold my peace and not defend myself, He would move. That very night, I turned on a Christian television program and heard an interview of a man that I had never seen or heard before or since. I do not remember his name but I remember his words. He spoke of Joseph in the Bible then related his personal experience of betrayal and hurt. He said the Lord spoke to his heart that *if he would hold his peace and not defend himself, that God would move for him.* I was stunned. I stared at the television in amazement. The Lord had made it abundantly clear to me that which I was NOT to do. I determined to do things His way though it was not always the easiest thing for my flesh.

There were many times I wondered if we would ever get beyond this season of pain and disappointment. My emotions were in control. I was in the middle of the worst battle of the mind I had ever faced. It was a barrage of why, what if, and why not. Each day I had to make myself get up, go through the daily routine when all I wanted to do was hide. I truly needed to be delivered.

We have always been people of prayer. God has been faithful and has moved for us time and again. He responds to the prayers of His children. However, I found myself in some kind of spiritual limbo. My prayers seemed to go unanswered. I *felt* forsaken though I knew in my heart that I belonged to the Lord. I did not sense His Presence, but I trusted that He was still with me. It was during this time that I struggled to pray. When I read the Bible, I could not seem to focus and retain what I read. I could be doing household chores and a floodgate of sadness would sweep over me. Recrimination followed me each day. The enemy of my soul constantly reminded me of my failure. He harassed me by telling me that God had let me down or since I did not measure up to expectations I had disappointed Him. It was one blow after another. Would God ever bless us again??

I simply came to the point of no longer wanting to fight any more battles. I had spiritual battle fatigue. I wanted to find a nice place to rest. From the beginning of my walk with the Lord years ago, He called me to be an intercessor. Now, I desperately needed someone to intercede for me. Thankfully, the Lord gave us dear friends who repeatedly prayed for us to get through this season.

Just when I would think all that hurt was behind me, something would bring it rushing back to my mind. I recall one particularly difficult night when I could not sleep and I was walking the floor and praying. It seemed like the night would never end. I longed for peace and rest. Terry awoke and came to the living room to check on me. Thank God for a husband who prays! He is my closest and most trusted intercessor. Terry held me and prayed. Soon he began singing hymns at the top of his voice. Somehow, hearing the words of those hymns sparked hope in my soul and I joined in song with him. It was important not only for God to hear me but for the enemy to hear me as well. Our faith was valid! It had not been destroyed, after all. We were singing from our heart that cold January night because the Lord was still real to us and not because circumstances changed. Regardless of how disappointed we had been, we knew our *only* answer was to trust the Lord. Our confidence would remain in our Deliverer and at just the right time, He *would* set us free from this sorrowful place. He would one day take us to a new place in Him, a deeper place in Him. Our faith had taken a beating, but deep within our hearts we continued to believe the Lord would turn our mourning into dancing (Psalm 30:11).

Our faith must matter, especially in the difficult times. It must matter beyond our feel good emotions. It must mean more than what I may receive from God's Hands. Our faith must mean an intimacy with Him through His Son, Jesus Christ that goes beyond the circumstances of life. It is this intimacy built over a lifetime that will sustain us when we cannot see how God is working in our behalf. Even when we feel our faith is low, we will know deep within our spirit that God remains faithful when others are not. That night as Terry and I sang to the Lord I wondered if the angels were part of the chorus, doing their part to strengthen me to rise above this torment. The Lord reminded me of Psalm 32: 7c where David writes that the Lord will surround him with songs of deliverance. The songs of the Lord encircled us that night to remind us He never leaves us nor forsakes us and will be with us until the end (Hebrews 13: 5c; Matthew 28: 20).

I could have given up on prayer. I could have given up on the Word of God. Deep within my heart I knew there was no giving up on the One Who had saved me and claimed me as His own. Even if I was unable to pray fervently at the moment or concentrate on scripture, then I would pray with weakness and read *something* from God's Word each day. Prayer is not about length or saying it like someone else but prayer is prayer when it comes from our heart in sincerity and earnestness. Jesus considered the seven word prayer of a tax collector that was prayed sincerely more effective than the longer prayer of the Pharisee who only recited his good works (Luke 18: 9-14). I also came to understand that when I read the Bible and only retain one word from the passage, that ONE word will enable me to stand and it has.

The important thing is to pray and read the Bible regardless of the storm we are traveling. This keeps us connected to our Source of strength. I had to be determined to stay connected to the Lord. I had to press in to Him, force my way through the blockades of the adversary and make my way into the throne room. When we are in the middle of the storm that is the time to get closer to the Lord and not pull away. When we continue to pray and read the Scriptures – even when the battle is raging and especially at this time - it is evident to the world, the flesh, and the devil that our lives are still submitted to the Sovereignty of God. Regardless of life's circumstances, He is still Lord. As Lord, He is in control whether it feels like it or looks like it in the natural realm. We could not see His Hand at work in all the turmoil to change things for us but that is when it is vitally important to continue to trust in His Plan that has yet to be unfolded. At times our knees may have been knocking but our feet remained firmly established upon the Rock.

As a result of our experience, the Lord has helped us to understand that people come into our lives for a season and a purpose but not always for the duration. Some are a part of our past, others a part of our present but not all of them together will be a part of our future. There will be divine connections in our lives and divine disconnections as well. We were reminded of Jonathan and David who bonded so close to one another. They were loyal to each other despite Jonathan's father, Saul, hating David to the point of attempting to murder him. Their close relationship was not life long due to Jonathan's death at the hand of the Philistines (I Samuel 31:2), but it was life affecting. Jonathan was not there when David became King of Israel, but David would always have memories of his dear friend. When we least expect it, there are some relationships in our lives that will be divinely disconnected from us. Instead of trying to put them back together, we should move on to what the Lord has for us in our future. When God changes a season in our lives, people are a part of that change. Our future season will have its own cast of people to play a role in the plan God has for us. This lesson came to us over time not overnight.

Chapter Ten

SURRENDER

It was during our struggle to come to grips with all that had happened, that I noticed something very strange had happened to me. It seemed that I had actually lost the desire to minister the Word of the Lord. To minister God's Word was something I had lived for, something I had found great joy in but that desire left me. After receiving the Baptism of the Holy Spirit in 1974, the Lord placed within me a hunger to learn the Scriptures. There is nothing that can impact a person's life as the Bible and for me to be able to share that Word with others was always a thrill and privilege. Yet, all of a sudden, the desire to minister the Word disappeared. I did not understand this. Was this from the Lord? Did *He* remove the desire for ministry from my heart? Did this mean that God really was through with me? Did He take His calling and anointing from my life? Had I so disappointed Him that He would never permit me to teach His Word again? The devil tried to convince me that this was exactly what had happened.

I was desperate for relief from the questions, the disappointments, losses, and pain. Human nature always wants a speedy deliverance, but God will not be rushed. Every circumstance of our lives has its own cycle to run, its own set course with a beginning, middle, and an end. The course has been determined and its purpose as well. God will use whatever means necessary to teach us truths from His Word and to teach us about Himself. He also seeks to teach us about ourselves. Bad, awful, heartbreaking, difficult, trying circumstances are not only about what the devil is attempting to do *to* us!!! They are also about that which the *Lord* wants to do *in* us.

However, I had become such a coward! When relief from our circumstances was slow in coming I earnestly prayed that the Lord would take me home. I wanted to be free of all the pain. I was so weary from it. Nonetheless, the Lord had other plans for my life and it did not include a premature exit. I had to get up and get on with life. God would not let me die, and He would not allow me the luxury of remaining a coward in His army. He would force this issue in my life to make me a strong warrior again, even in the broken places.

He *made* me live in spite of myself, the circumstances and especially in spite of the devil. Early on in the crisis, the Lord gave me the Scripture in Psalms 118: 17 which says "I shall not die, but live, and declare the works of the Lord." A few days after He gave me this promise, Terry and I attended a service at Trinity Chapel Church of God in Powder Springs, Georgia, to hear Darlene Bishop. When she began her message, her text was "I shall not die, but live, and declare the works of the Lord." His Word was confirmed to my heart. God was determined to bring this Scripture to pass in my life. He held me up so I could stand on the Word and not give up. He set me on the Rock! (Psalm 40: 2b) When I thought my feet were surely slipping, His mercy held me up! (Psalm 94: 18)

The psalmist knew weakness. He knew his limitations and he knew he had to rely on God. No matter how "spiritually together" we think we are, we are still jars of clay (II Corinthians 4: 7) that can break under the right pressure. We need the Lord to hold us together. I am so thankful that He truly kept me together because I was not capable of doing it myself. When I did not have the strength to stand, and when I did not want to stand or to try any more, the *Lord Jesus* stood up in me and caused me to stand. There were times that I confessed the Scripture over my life in a whisper because my strength and spirit was so low. I am here today because the sheer power of the Word of God spoken only in a whisper is sufficient to bring about a miracle.

I came to learn that this season of being sidelined from a teaching ministry was only temporary. The greater purpose was restoration and healing for body and spirit. The Lord taught me that it was only an "interruption" in ministry and not a removal from ministry. God allows and sometimes sends interruptions into our lives for a specific purpose that He will reveal in due time. When interruptions accomplish good and lasting results in our lives, we should not consider them as negative.

The Lord did not stop using me. He simply used me in other ways than from behind a podium. He would have people call me to pray with them, and He would give me scriptures to encourage them. I confess that many times I would think to myself that I am the one that is in need of prayer! Nevertheless, the Lord would anoint me to pray and speak a Word into the person's life. I could hardly pray for myself; yet, here I was, praying for others. This always amazed me *and* assured me that the Lord was not finished with me. The Lord was proving to me that He was infinitely greater in me than I understood.

I believe we open the door to our own healing when we are willing to minister or help someone else even when our own need is great. I was being used on a smaller scale but I was thankful for it. Romans 11:29 reminded me, "For the gifts and calling of God are without repentance." The Word was the truth of the matter. God had not cancelled His calling on my life even though the venue and structure had changed. Regardless of changes around us or in us, God remains the same. Complete restoration to my purpose in the Kingdom of God would take time and by way of His chosen path of healing for me.

As the days and months went by, the Lord was slowly and deliberately renewing my life. I cannot explain why the Lord chose to do it this way but His plan would be accomplished in the manner He determined. The more renewal I experienced, the more I realized that I was sensing the desire to teach again. Would my perceived failure in one arena prevent me from ever stepping into another? Should I plead with the Lord to use me again? Or should I just forget it and let it be a fond memory? I came to the place called Surrender.

In Genesis 22, the Lord gives specific instructions to Abraham to take his son, Isaac, and sacrifice him on an altar. Abraham obeyed without fanfare, without tears and without delay. He knew there was a promise over Isaac's life. If he had to sacrifice him to please the Lord, then he would trust the Lord to raise him up in order for the promise to come to pass. The One who makes the promise is the same One who keeps the promise. There are some things that are out of our hands to accomplish and bringing the Promises of God to pass is certainly one of them. That is under the control of the sovereignty of God. Anything flesh can do to bring it to pass will fail miserably.

Abraham surrendered his son on the altar in obedience and worship not in regret or dismay. Isaac was the son of the Promise! He was not the son who was a result of man but a miracle from God. Now, Abraham needed another miracle. He knew the Lord had provided in other ways in the past, and he trusted God would make a way again. First, he had to let go of his dearly loved son. When Abraham surrendered, he did just that. He literally took his hands off and in doing so he was saying it is all up to the Lord now. If he had not taken his hands off the son he loved and cherished, it would not have been *complete* surrender.

I came to the place of surrender, my own personal altar, and I laid my ministry at the Cross. I let go. I took my hands off and left it at His feet. If the Lord was ready for my ministry to close and I had given my last message, then so be it. It was all in His Hands. Ministry is God's business. He can employ whom He chooses, and He can retire whom He chooses. I decided to ask Him to help me be the best Christian woman I could be and not concern myself with ministry opportunities. The most important thing is for me to be like Christ in this world. If the Lord chose to bury or to resurrect my ministry, it was totally up to Him. I determined not to try to "make" things happen. It would be up to the Lord to supernaturally open any future ministry door. I wanted Him most of all. Everything else takes a back seat. If His plans for my life involved ministry again, then His hands were big enough to sovereignly open those doors without me lifting a finger. *In His time*, He did exactly that. After I was much stronger and in better health, amazing opportunities for ministry came without any effort on my part. The Lord used the awful storm I experienced to propel me into other areas of ministry that I would not have had otherwise.

Before He opened those new doors for me, He set me aside for healing and perfecting. I did not say perfection but perfecting. I have not arrived, but God continues the deliberate maturing process of transforming me into the image of His Son. The process can be most uncomfortable but the rewards are everlasting.

The Lord gave me understanding that the fervent desire I had in the past to minister His Word was lifted only for a season so that I could be still and simply get well. This was the goodness and kindness of God my Father and not His anger or displeasure. At one point in my season of healing, the Lord spoke to my heart that I mean more to Him than any ministry. I have to confess that I was shocked when I heard those words. I was astounded and thought to myself – I do?? I thought ministry meant everything to the Lord. What a joy to realize that it is me instead! How liberating! I had the misconception that church was at the top of God's list of priorities when it is actually you and me. After all, Christ came for people! The Father loved the world so much that He sent His only begotten Son to give His life for us (John 3:16). How great is His love toward us! (I John 3:1) He paid an awesome price for our souls and love was His motivation.

I learned through this difficult season that pain is an equalizer no matter the direction from which it comes. It is one thing that places us all on the same level regardless of our position in life. No one can escape it. The difference is only in the degrees of pain that some experience. Pain is a schoolmaster that teaches us what joy does not. It has the capacity to teach us compassion for others unless we allow pain to make us bitter. If this occurs, then we are only sorry for ourselves and not for others. The more compassion we have, the less *self*-conscious we are and the more *people* conscious we become. Compassion will move us to respond to others in need without hesitation or criticism but with loving-kindness.

I believe this is the picture we see in the Good Samaritan in Luke 10: 25-37. The Good Samaritan focused on getting the injured man well and was willing to do whatever it took to see it happen. If the Good Samaritan had listened only with his ears, he may have become judgmental and self righteous. He may have left the man to pull himself up by his own sandals, just as the priest and Levite did. The example of the Samaritan causes me to wonder if perhaps he had faced a similar circumstance in his own life and knew how it felt to be beaten, wounded, robbed and left to die. Maybe those same religious leaders passed him by as well. Perhaps he determined that he would never treat anyone with such unconcern and disrespect. He learned compassion and then extended it to someone else in pain. The manner in which he learned compassion is really unknown to us. It may have stemmed from an experience in his past that prompted him to reach out to the traveler that day and *do* something for him. He was a good student of pain because it caused him to move into action and to minister to someone else. This is the reward of painful experiences.

To love the Lord with all our heart, soul, mind, and strength and our neighbor as we love ourselves (Mark 12: 30-31) *must* mean something more than responding as the religious leaders did. It means mercy will triumph over the *cause* of the person's injury, and look beyond the possible failures of the wounded, and lend support for that person to be well again. We will listen with our hearts not just our ears. When we do, we will better understand how we can help them recover.

Each of us travels our own journey of faith in this life. Even though there will be difficulties as we do, it is the only road worth traveling. The gains far outweigh the losses. II Corinthians 4: 16-18 (NIV) promises us: "Therefore we do not lose heart. Though outwardly we are wasting away, yet inwardly we are being renewed day by day. For our light and momentary troubles are achieving for us an eternal glory that far outweighs them all. So we fix our eyes not on what is seen but on what is unseen. For what is seen is temporary, but what is unseen is eternal." I am sure eternity holds many rewards for the redeemed, but Christ is the supreme reward, the One that is above all others. When our heart is fixed on Him, we know there is nothing and no one more important than our relationship with Christ. He wants and deserves to be first in our hearts, above ministry, relationships, possessions, or anything of this earthly existence. I never want ministry to be my reason for living. I want it to be Jesus.

Chapter Eleven

WORSHIP IS A DECISION

In the 1970's and 80's we lived in another city and were members at Mount Paran Church of God in Atlanta, Georgia. At that time, Dr. Paul L. Walker was the senior pastor and Dr. M. G. McLuhan was the associate pastor. They gave us a strong foundation in the Word of God to which we continue to holdfast. That foundation kept us anchored during this very low point in our lives. Even when things looked bleak and our faith seemed so small, we still trusted that God would somehow bring good from the awful mess we had been through. When we had no answers to our many questions that mustard seed of faith remained in our hearts because "we knew that we knew" the Word of God could not fail. Even if we felt like *we* had failed.

The enemy sought to destroy all our hope in God, but he would not succeed. We know the Word is true if nothing and no one else is, and at some point, we would see His goodness in the land of the living (Psalm 27: 13). We would wait on God. This is not *easy* to do. It is only easy to *say*. This is especially true when all you see is opposite of your faith and hope in Him. Trusting in the Lord is not about being *easy*. It is about having confidence in His wisdom and in His kindness to bring the answer we need. It may not always be the answer we *want*. Faith will praise Him regardless because it will be the *right* answer.

At this point in our lives it seemed natural to return to Mount Paran to be renewed and refreshed. It was the right answer for us from the Lord. It was the Sovereign Hand of God taking us back to our spiritual home. There has always been a marvelous spirit of worship there along with anointed preaching and teaching. In spite of what had happened, our humiliation and feeling like a failure, we knew returning to that kind of spiritual environment and joining in the worship would be spiritual medicine for our lives.

The choir and orchestra always lifted our spirit into the Presence of the Lord and we found such solace. There were times I thought there is no earthly reason to be worshipping because nothing about our situation has really changed. My health problems became even worse but we worshipped. We made a quality decision to worship the Lord regardless of unanswered questions, regardless of our broken hearts, and regardless of the actions of any human being. God was still God and He was still good. He deserved worship. A worshipper of the Lord will not be defeated. A worshipper may get knocked down in life but he or she will worship until they are standing once again.

There was one Sunday morning service I recall that as I *worshipped* I could sense His Presence in a very special way. It was as if there was no one else in the world but Him and me. It was like being in a spiritual vacuum that was filled with God's glory. I was His, He was mine. No outside circumstance can change that. When His Presence filled my heart so completely, all the broken pieces began to come together.

We had not given up on the Lord, and He had not given up on us. No matter how long we must wait to see our miracle come to pass, we will see it in due season. Galatians 6:9 (NKJV) tells us "And let us not grow weary while doing good, for in due season we shall reap if we do not lose heart." Due season is just a matter of time.

The ministry of the choir and orchestra, under the direction of Mark Blankenship, has been a healing balm to our spirit. The impact of this ministry on our lives cannot be measured. They never failed to minister to the depth of our being and to lift us above the sadness. It was remarkable how the Lord used this ministry every single service.

Dr. Walker retired as pastor many years ago and for the last several years Dr. David Cooper has pastored Mount Paran. His ministry has been heaven sent to us. Every Sunday the Lord would give him just the right message for *us*. We were amazed at the goodness of the Lord. With every message we heard came another degree of deliverance. Our mind was being renewed and our spirit restored. We were exactly where we needed to be. During the week we would look forward to the next service with such anticipation for the message the Lord would give to us. It was our lifeline to wholeness again. We believe our healing would not have happened as quickly if we had not submitted ourselves to scriptural preaching and teaching and involved ourselves in worship. It is totally possible that a root of bitterness could have overtaken our lives instead of experiencing a glorious healing.

We were so thrilled to be back at Mount Paran and reacquaint ourselves with people we had not seen in years. One Sunday morning after we had been to the altar for prayer, Bill Bailey, a long time member of Mount Paran, embraced Terry and told him "welcome back home!" That simple phrase spoken in love meant so much to Terry. He did feel welcomed and we both appreciated his prayers for us. We are very thankful for every prayer we received each time we walked the church aisle to be anointed with oil and prayed for by a church elder. With every prayer, His Presence ministered to us. Another familiar face was Larry Owens who often reached out with a handshake or a hug or a prayer to let us know he was glad we were home. These simple gestures were so meaningful to us.

Since it is a large church, it is good to get connected with others in smaller care groups or in a class. We were leaving church one Sunday morning when I realized Terry and I had gotten separated in the crowd. I looked for him and he was talking with Jim and Kay Moss, who happen to be two of the dearest people on the planet. Terry and Jim were prayer partners at the men's prayer breakfast years ago. When I saw who Terry was speaking with, I was overjoyed. I joined them in conversation and Kay invited us to the Bible study class they. We did not attend that morning but we did soon thereafter.

After going through the experience we had, we were a little hesitant about getting close to people again. It was easier to withdraw. However, when we visited the class, we felt at home right away. Everyone in the class was warm and genuine. It was apparent that the class cared for each other and for us too. It was easy to see that the people in this class had the love of God in their hearts and were willing to share it with others. When they learned of my health problems, they earnestly prayed for me on several occasions. They had no way of knowing that God was using them to take us by the hand and slowly but surely lift us from the shadows. We thank the Lord for letting us see Jim and Kay that morning and introducing us to these special people. Each one in the class is a jewel and we thank the Lord for allowing us to walk into class that Sunday morning and find hearts that reached out and welcomed us as one of their own. We were amazed that we sensed no rejection from them and they actually wanted us to be a part of the class! We will always cherish this marvelous group of people who reached out to hurting people – without knowing it - and loved them as they were.

This class, along with the music ministry, and the pastoral preaching was the oil and the wine God used to pour healing into our lives. This is precisely what the Great Physician ordered for us. The Lord had orchestrated our return to Mount Paran, placing people in our lives that were instrumental in our renewal. The goodness of the Lord is so obvious.

There were other steps *I* would have to take as well to see my healing come fully. These steps would include additional life-changing decisions I would have to make that would affect not only my life but others.

Chapter Twelve

THE FINAL BRIDGE TO MY HEALING

In December 2005 I was feeling much stronger physically. I thought my healing was finally here. Then in January 2006 I had a setback. I actually felt like I was being poisoned throughout my system. I thought this just might be the time the Lord actually takes me home but He had another plan. One morning when I reached for the medicine I had been taking the Lord clearly spoke to my heart, "*This* is what is making you sick." I never took that medicine again. However, the negative effect it had on my system took a while to get over. There were times I wondered if I ever would. It seemed a slow recovery but at least I was no longer being poisoned by the wrong medicine. While medicine can play an important role in good health, the wrong medicine can be deadly. Fortunately, soon after stopping the wrong medicine, a very caring and insightful physician prescribed the appropriate medicine for me that worked extremely well.

The change in medicine was not all I needed. The Lord's plan for me to be restored to health and wholeness included teaching me the necessary steps I would have to take to be well again. Healing is not about God's miraculous power alone. It is also about personal responsibility. There are some things I am required to do. Healing then becomes a partnership with God to experience the best health possible. Obedience to His Word is the key to victory in every situation. Soon I would be given the choice for victory once and for all.

While medicine was beneficial to my health, it could not bring complete healing to me. The next phase of my healing would not result from a doctor's prescription but through very special people which God selected for this purpose. He ordained divine appointments for me with each one. Over a year's time, these divine appointments would be God's way of building the bridge that was the means of my deliverance. He worked in divine order, a divine pattern of "Precept upon precept, line upon line" (Isaiah 28:10). He has the complete pattern in view where we see only a portion at a time. We continue to walk by faith and to trust that His pattern will be unveiled as needed, being assured it is a good pattern. Jeremiah 29: 11 (NIV) says "For I know the plans I have for you, declares the Lord, plans to prosper you and not to harm you, plans to give you hope and a future."

I have never been a very good seamstress though my Mother was. I have sewn enough to know that without a good pattern, your work is haphazard and probably will be disastrous. Actually, my sewing is pretty much a disaster *with* a pattern. God's pattern for our lives is perfect for us as individuals and will always result in something good if we live by it. He never loses sight of what He has ordained for our lives. This does not mean that He uses only bright colors for the pattern. He will use the dark ones, the subtle ones and those that get a person's attention. The design of our lives become a balance of hope, faith, humility, lessons learned, victories won, crushing defeats, joyful successes, untrustworthy flesh, but a faithful God.

Our greatest problems arise when we take His pattern and try to adjust it to suit ourselves. That is willful rebellion. The outcome will be a colossal mess on our hands. Thankfully, the mercy and the love of God are always available to clean us up, correct us, and set us on our feet to get back in the swing of things – His way. He never throws away the pattern.

Over the years the Lord has given me a few close friends who are simply the best. They are people who are genuine and trustworthy. Each was included in the perfect pattern that God had designed to restore me. The first three, Sarah Lee (whom we affectionately call Tiny), Vera Ferguson and Rhonda Lee, are women I have had an enduring friendship for over thirty years. We are prayer partners as well, having prayed over countless circumstances of life. We have seen the Lord move so many times in answer to our prayers. We have stood together to face whatever came our way. If one of us had a problem, we all had a problem. We bore one another's burdens. Many times when one of us needed special prayer we would do whatever was necessary to get together for prayer. There is great power in agreement that is based on the Word of God. We would use the anointing oil and call on the Lord of Glory. We would leave our prayer gatherings with the assurance that God had met with us and heard our fervent cry. We knew the answer was on the way.

One morning in January 2006 I needed one of those meetings to take place. Rhonda called to see how I was doing. The truth was I was not doing well at all. I was in awful shape and Rhonda recognized it right away. Before the morning was over, she and Vera were in my living room ready to pray for me. I was thankful beyond words. Help had arrived but I would be surprised with the form it would take.

Rhonda and Vera came with a determination to see a breakthrough. They prayed as only friends can pray – earnestly, and with genuine love and concern. They prayed for me as if they were praying for themselves. I sat on the sofa and Vera slipped her arm around me letting me rest my head on her shoulder. I was very weak. Then she gave me a word of instruction from the Lord. She told me I needed to go to the people who had hurt me and to tell them that I forgive them. She told me that in order for me to truly get well, this was something I had to do. *Oops.* I had not planned on that being part of the equation for me to receive my healing! I had expected the Lord's healing touch not this! I had told the Lord many times that I had forgiven those who hurt us. I asked Him to bless them, but He wanted me to take it a step further. Rhonda was in agreement and I trusted in the counsel of my friends. This was not a comfortable position but I was willing to take this step of obedience to please the Lord and for me to be healed. When we want something enough, we will do whatever it takes to see it become a reality. I wanted to be well and I wanted everything to be right between Him and me. I also wanted everything to be right between others and myself. I would need Him to show me how and when to handle this.

When I awoke the next morning, I knew this was the day I had to follow through on the counsel my friends had given me. I sensed His grace in my heart to accomplish His will. Vera had offered to go with me but I did not feel I could wait. Since she lives some distance from me, it could be several days before she could come again. That morning, I had to make the necessary phone calls. I believed I was ready to do this. There would be no turning back.

I sat at my desk and asked the Lord to give me the words to say and as He did, I wrote them down. I made the phone calls and all parties were home that morning. I expressed to them that even though I did not understand why they hurt the church and us, I loved them and I forgave them. I asked them to forgive me for hurting them in anyway. It was time for all of us to move on in the direction the Lord would lead us. I had a wonderful conversation with each of them. One of the people I called told me that just that week she had written to Terry and me expressing a desire to resolve everything, but she had not mailed it. Later she did so. God was working on all hearts.

Once I made the decision to do the right thing, there was a God-given strength to get it done. If ever I have been submitted to the Spirit, it was that morning. When I finished the calls, I had a joy in my heart that was like a celebration. I was so thankful that He enabled me to do something that was very difficult for me. I began praising the Lord as I walked through my home. I do not know when I have ever been so glad I was saved. The Lord was real to me that morning. *He proved to me that He was bigger than my hurt and sickness and anything else in this entire world!*

Later that morning I called another prayer partner, who had been a member of our church, Jean Holcombe. Jean and I developed a close friendship soon after she began attending our church. We have spent many hours in prayer and have testimonies of the Lord answering. On this particular morning I invited her to my home because I wanted to tell her face to face what a great thing the Lord had done for me. When she arrived, I shared my testimony of the morning's events. She was amazed at the greatness of the Lord that enabled me to do the right thing. She felt a release in her heart from the hurt of it all as well. At one point, the Lord gave me a vision: I saw Christ seated at the right Hand of God the Father and He nodded to the Father and looked at me and smiled. It was if He was saying "good girl!" I knew in my heart He was pleased that I had done the right thing even when it was difficult.

Jean sat with me for a good while as I rested. It had been an eventful morning, to say the least. I knew healing was on its way. I wanted it for everyone not just me!

Of course at the time all this transpired I did not consider how the Lord had been building the bridge for my recovery even before January. He had already placed in our lives established friendships that would be there for us during this time and each one was a vital link in our deliverance.

A very dear couple in our lives is Margaret and Robert Sampson. Margaret and I have been close for over thirty-eight years. We have weathered many storms together and our loyalty to each other is steadfast. We have wept through life's difficult times and laughed ourselves silly through the good ones. Proverbs 17: 17 NKJV tells us, "A friend loves at all times, and a brother is born for adversity." Being a friend to someone in the worst of times proves the depth of the relationship. Margaret and Robert weathered our storm with us. They never ceased believing in us when it was difficult for *us* to do so. In the many hours of conversation we had they always focused on the positive, reminding us of God's purpose in our lives. They refused to let us accept the garbage that Satan dumped on us. They listened to us with their hearts, cried with us, advised us and let us lean on them. They were there for us whenever we needed them and we need our dear friends *always*.

We have "long distance" friends as well. Patti and Carl Heiselman live in Oklahoma but this does not affect our closeness as friends. No matter where they live, their friendship is an essential part of our lives. They stood in their authority as believers and proclaimed victory to our lives and ministry. They would not accept anything less. Patti said many times that this would be a promotion for us. I never wanted to admit to her that it did not seem possible. They would never let us give up on our calling and purpose in God. Patti would not allow me to wallow in my sorrow, no matter how hard I tried!! They are our Aaron and Hur holding up our arms in the battle. Joshua and his men won that war, remember? (Exodus 17: 8-14) We win also because our friends gave of their strength to us.

The enemy did not want to give up too easily. His plan was to harass us and wear us down. Even though the oppression was not as bad as it had been months before, I still found myself dealing with unanswered questions. It was hard to let go. By April I was doing much better physically but the battle of the mind was proving the most difficult battle of all.

Early one Saturday morning, I sensed such an eerie heaviness invade my life. It was an oppression that I had never known before. I knew the source and I knew I had to have deliverance that day. I wanted victory once and for all. I had to get in touch with the Lord myself. I could not wait for Terry to get home from work and it was too early to call a prayer partner. I wondered to myself exactly how to pray. I bowed on my knees in the living room and cried out to the Lord for deliverance. I did not make a great lengthy prayer or get into heavy spiritual warfare. This was between the Lord and me. I prayed a simple prayer from my heart. As I knelt before the Lord, I told Him that I had to have His help *that* morning. I stood on the Word from James 4:7 and prayed "I submit myself to You and I resist the devil and he must flee". I also told Him that I had loved Him since I was a little girl and that would never change regardless of any circumstance of life or any spiritual foe that was determined to destroy me. I belong to Him and I trust Him to help me. In that moment, God delivered me. I stood up and I was set free. God touched me right there, right then. How big is God?? He is big enough. When you belong to Him, He is there for you.

As time went on, it was becoming easier to see that God was redeeming the difficult experience we had been through. Our joy and peace were being restored. Even though all our questions have not been answered (and they never will be), our hope remains in God. It is all in God's Hands just as we are.

There was one more divine appointment I needed to keep. Seldom do I go to the grocery store on Saturdays. I really try to avoid it. However, one Saturday in June I needed to do just that. I had been cleaning house and I looked like a haint. I am not sure exactly what a haint looks like but I am positive it is not good. I just knew that I looked the part whether I could define it or not. Hopefully no one I knew would see me. As I rushed through the aisles, I turned and there was Bea Rountree, the wife of Rev. Glenn Rountree who pastors West Metro Church of God in Douglasville, Georgia. This just could not be happening! I wondered if the Lord was having a good chuckle over this. There was nothing I could hide behind. Soup cans do not make a good cover. Like it or not, all my "hainthood" was for all to see, including this beautiful sister in Christ. I had not seen Bea in a very long time and she looked just wonderful – *as usual*! Could she not look really terrible at least this once!! Apparently not. (I suppose "hainthood" – as misery - loves company.)

Bea's spirit shines through her countenance and only intensifies her natural beauty. She is the kind of person that makes you feel better just by being around her. You would think that as soon as she saw me she would drop to her knees and begin praying for me since I looked so terrible. She had to know there was something seriously wrong! (At least I hope she did.) Bea looked past how I looked and stopped to talk with me a moment. She knew in her heart that our meeting was not an accident, and that God had something in mind, and I realized it as well. I decided I might as well forget my hair going in different directions and no makeup and attempt to hear from the Lord in this meeting.

Bea asked me how our church was doing. I told her it had been the most wonderful experience we had ever had but became the most awful without spelling out any details. She began ministering to me right there on aisle three. She shared with me from their experience many years ago at another church they had pastored. Believe it or not, their experience was identical to ours. As she ministered to me I sensed the presence of the Lord and she did as well. We were unconcerned for all the customers walking by for we were in the middle of a God-ordained meeting. She imparted wisdom, love, and concern which are a spiritual combination that can not be matched. Before seeing Bea that day, Terry and I had desired that we would have an opportunity to talk with other pastors that had been through a similar situation. Our hope was to learn from them. God answered in His sovereign way. Bea completely understood how we felt and she had no judgmental attitude or criticism of us. She listened with her heart. Sometime later, we visited in their home for dinner and fellowship that was free of us finger pointing. We were there for the right reasons. They prayed with us and encouraged us with a word that the Lord had given Pastor Rountree years before: God does not waste pain and we should not waste our sorrows. This time of sharing with the Rountree's gave us more hope than ever. Our future was looking brighter. Finally, we could see there *was* light at the end of this long tunnel. We will always remember their kindness to us and the hope they conveyed.

We had several occasions to visit with Bea and Pastor Glenn in their church. During one of those services, the Lord ministered to Terry in a very special way regarding all the hurt he experienced from our loss. The Lord gave Terry a vision of an old model car that had a rear luggage rack with straps to hold the luggage in place. As Terry saw this vision, the Lord spoke to his heart concerning its meaning to his own life. The Lord spoke to Terry's heart and asked him: "you see the car with the luggage strapped on?" Yes, he saw it all right. Terry knew in his spirit that the car represented him carrying unnecessary baggage that was filled with hurt and disappointment from the painful experience. The Lord instructed him: "cut those straps, let the baggage drop off and do not look back." At that moment, in the Presence of the Lord, Terry let it all go and he sensed the release in his spirit. He has not looked back. None of us can go forward with the future God has for us if we hold tightly to the cumbersome baggage of the past and allow it to control our lives. We must choose to "cut those straps", release all the baggage, and never look back. Thank God, Terry and I have made this choice. Healing was being released in our lives.

Chapter Thirteen

WHEN MORNING CAME

Even though I am near the end of this book, I can say there is no end to the lessons the Lord continues to teach us from our loss and seeming failure. In that regard, the story continues. When we were walking through those dark days, I never thought I would see anything good as a result. That is how the enemy wanted me to see things. At the time, I simply could not envision any good coming from all the pain, but that is exactly what the Lord has done. He is so amazing! He has brought much good into our lives as a result of the *trial*. Blessings did not do that. A gut wrenching trial did! He has added much more to our lives than was ever taken. If I attempted to list all the Lord has done for us through this experience, I can assure you it would be a long one. I can say with certainty that the Lord has poured more into our lives than we ever lost. We understand that He is *always* with us regardless of circumstances of life. We have discovered that when we walk through difficult places and holdfast to Him and His Word nonetheless, He blesses us with a greater sense of His Presence in our lives than we have ever experienced. This alone has made it all worthwhile for us.

I can never praise Him enough for not allowing this vessel to *remain* broken. For a very long time all I could see was my life in fragments. He brought wholeness and function to my life again using many wonderful people along with His glorious grace and His Word. He alone poured more of His presence into my life that sealed each fragment.

Our journey of faith did not end in a terrible abyss of failure and disappointment! It could not because we belong to God. Pure and simple. He would never leave us in such a place. This "rough spot" we traveled was only a small portion of our life's journey with Christ. Our destination is still in view and Christ is leading the way.

Terry and I held on to the Lord and He held onto us to bring us through. Yes, at times we did not "feel" that we would ever get through this. Some days seemed so long and the nights were even longer. Everything has its own duration and there were no quick solutions and no easy departures. The Lord was taking us through the process one day at a time. We held on the truth that we "knew" in Whom we had believed and His Word could not fail us. It is a lamp unto our feet and the light to our pathway (Psalm 119: 105). The light of the Word was pointing us in the right direction.

There are no magic formulas in the Kingdom of God to escape the circumstances of life. There is only faith in God, the Blood of Christ, His power and His Word. When you are sinking in rough waters, it will not be a formula you grasp. All that matters at that point, and always, is your relationship with the Lord and your foundation in the Word of God. When we trust Him, He will take hold of us and cause us to rise above the waves and live. He was always walking with us, never against us, to ensure our survival. At times in all probability He carried Terry and me. Even though He sent many wonderful people who ministered to us in countless ways, it was the Lord Himself Who was close beside us in the midnight hour to sustain us till morning light. Weeping endured for a time, but joy came in the morning and when it did, strength came also. (Psalm 30:5; Nehemiah 8:10)

This experience has taught me in a deeper way than ever before – it is never over until God says it is over. Regardless of the enemy's plots against us, God would not let this circumstance be the end for us. It was not the final chapter of our lives or our ministry.

Restoration takes time. It took over a year and a half for my health to rebound and my spirit to be renewed. God has blessed us not only to survive but to do so with joy. We have weathered the winds and waves. The enemy's goal was to use the storm to permanently take us out. But – if God be for us, who can be against us? (Romans 8: 31b) The *Lord's* purpose will stand in our lives. *He* always knew we would make it through this dark tempest.

It has been made so clear to us that God has ordained His church to function as a body ministry and care for one another. We have witnessed the Lord blending gifts from so many in His body to bring healing to our lives. He meshed our old friends and new friends to fortify and hold us up in prayer and counsel and we cherish each one. He placed us in a powerful church ministry where worship was pure and unto Him, and to reinforce the truth of His Word in our hearts.

Ministry within the Body of Christ is fulfilled in every day living also. Ken Hatcher, Terry's business associate and good friend, would stop by on business and have prayer with Terry and encourage him. I also had a conversation with Ken by telephone one day that was extremely helpful to me as I was getting well. Terry and I appreciate Ken's prayers and concern during this season of recovery. Jesus uses willing vessels in all walks of life to reflect His love and nature. It is not always the grand gesture that accomplishes this, but oftentimes it is the unseen kindness that is extended with genuine consideration.

Mark 12: 30-31 NKJV records the words of Jesus: "... you shall love the Lord your God with all your heart, with all your soul, with all your mind, and with all your strength. This is the first commandment. And the second, like it, is this: You shall love your neighbor as yourself. There is no other commandment greater than these." These words of Jesus establish the priority for us His followers – loving Him, loving others. Love remains the hallmark for Christianity and always will. Jesus said in John 13: 35 (NIV) "By this all men will know that you are my disciples, if you love one another."

Chapter Fourteen

EARTHEN VESSELS

Jesus could have fulfilled His ministry on earth without calling men to be His disciples, men who would give Him problems along the way. Instead, the plan of God included Christ choosing flawed, imperfect people who often misinterpreted His mission and misunderstood Him. These men were the very ones He determined to be the foundation of His church. He delegated His authority and His mission to this diverse group of men who were pretty rough around the edges. He chose the likes of brash Peter; and the rowdy brothers, James and John; Matthew, a heartless tax collector; along with Peter's brother Andrew; Philip; Bartholomew; Thomas (who might not make it today in any faith movement!); James; Thaddeus; Simon the Canaanite; and Judas Iscariot who betrayed Christ. With the exception of Judas Iscariot, these impetuous men are the ones the Lord used to "turn the world upside down." (Acts 17: 6c)

These men would not have been singled out by the Pharisees or Sadducees to be the apostles of the early church. Yet, Jesus did. He saw value and potential in each person He called, just as He sees value and potential in all of us. God's plan has always been to have a church on the earth that would continue the work of Christ by the power of His Spirit.

This supernaturally empowered organism is to advance the Kingdom of God, using the gifts He has placed within the Body. These gifts are vitally important for public ministry and also one on one. When there is an area of the Body that is wounded or injured, He wants the Body to care for itself with these gifts (I Corinthians 12: 18-27). We rejoice with those that rejoice and weep with those that weep (Romans 12: 15). We are all in the same boat and we need each other to get to the other side.

Time after time, the Lord used gifted friends to minister to us and to help us get beyond the place of wounding and sorrow. Each one reinforced to our hearts what the Word declares about whom we are in Christ and to whom we belong. The opinion of the devil does not matter. They always reminded us that the devil is and always will be a liar. In our heart-to-heart discussions, they were honest and straightforward with our best interests at heart. They did not sugar-coat anything. Terry and I will always be grateful for each person the Lord used to lift us and strengthen us to move on.

God has proven how great He is in us. It was not a matter of Him being on the seashore watching as a spectator wondering how or if we would make it. He always knew we would because He was in the boat with us, keeping us secure. He has caused us to stand in His grace and faith. Our foundation has proven to be built on the solid Rock, Christ Jesus.

We all are jars of clay. The Treasure is within and from Him. The vessel may suffer injury at times, but in the Hands of the Potter the brokenness is totally repairable. In Jeremiah 18 the Lord instructed the prophet to go down to the potter's house. God wanted His prophet to hear His words as Jeremiah watched the work the potter was accomplishing on his wheel. The potter had a particular purpose in mind for the vessel but evidently, a flaw appeared in the process and the potter could not let that remain. He would not abandon the vessel or the process because of an imperfection. Just the right pressure was applied to remove it. Scripture does not tell us if the flaw was external or internal, carnal or spiritual, but the potter has the ability to see either and the power to bring remedy. As Jeremiah looked on, the Lord asked the question: "O house of Israel, can I not do with you as this potter?" God answers the question Himself: "Look, as the clay is in the potter's hand, so are you in My hand, O house of Israel!" (NKJV) Yes, indeed, we are in the glorious hands of the master Potter.

While the Lord see us as we really are, He also sees us as we could be as a result of His handiwork. The process is not without compassion. Hebrews 4: 14 – 16 NIV assures us: "Therefore, since we have a great high priest who has gone through the heavens, Jesus the Son of God, let us hold firmly to the faith we profess. For we do not have a high priest who is unable to sympathize with our weaknesses, but we have One who has been tempted in every way, just was we are- yet was without sin. Let us then approach the throne of grace with confidence so that we may receive mercy and find grace to help us in our time of need." If someone has sympathy or understanding for others there will be no condemnation toward them. Christ Jesus is such a Savior and High Priest. He welcomes us to the throne of grace, extending mercy for our condition and grace to stand. No flaw or imperfection or any broken area in the vessel will ever change the fact that the vessel is still chosen for the Potter's purpose. He will reshape it and make it a vessel of honor.

The Lord does not abandon us because we are weak, imperfect clay vessels. He knew that when He called us unto Himself. He will complete the good work He has begun in us (Philippians 1:6). No season of brokenness will prevent this work from being finished. Once again, the Lord has proven Himself faithful. The enemy did not have the last word over our lives after all. God would never allow that. His sovereignty will always have the last word and it is not defeat. It is victory. Romans 8: 33-39 (NKJV) assures us: "Who will bring any charge against those whom God has chosen? It is God who justifies. Who is he that condemns? Christ Jesus, who died – more than that, who was raised to life – is at the right Hand of God and is also interceding for us. Who shall separate us from the love of Christ? Shall trouble or hardship or persecution or famine or nakedness or danger or sword? As it is written: For your sake we face death all day long; we are considered as sheep to be slaughtered. No, in all these things we are more than conquerors through Him who loved us. For I am convinced that neither death nor life, neither angels nor demons, neither the present nor the future, nor any powers, neither height nor depth, nor anything else in all creation, will be able to separate us from the love of God that is in Christ Jesus our Lord." As a child of God, we triumph over the storm, adversity, difficulty, loss, failure, disappointment, brokenness, even demonic forces - because His victory is ours. We can claim it in every circumstance that life dishes out. This victory was secured for us at Calvary through the perfect sacrifice of Christ Jesus, the holy Lamb of God. No weapon, no wicked plot, no lie of the devil, no physical, mental, emotional or spiritual attack, no assault of any design can ever defeat this victory. It cannot be stolen or overtaken or minimized in our lives. We need only to believe. It may take a brief time or it may take an extended season for us to experience our victory in the natural realm especially as circumstances are screaming defeat. But when the storm has passed and the dust has settled, we will be standing in His might and strength. We win indeed!

REMEMBER

I have shared with you my testimony of the goodness of God at work in the lives of two people who love Him with all their heart. I hope it has ministered to you. God is bigger than any hurt that you have experienced in your life. I want you to remember that His goodness has nothing to do with the circumstances you face in this life. The Lord's love never fades. Circumstances come and go just as people may, but His love is permanent. Whatever your circumstances, whatever area of brokenness you may have in your life, whatever burdens you have today, remember that He cares for you. He is only a prayer away. He can change circumstances and people. He can heal brokenness and lift heavy burdens.

If you do not know the reality of your sins being forgiven and being assured of going to heaven after this life is passed, please call on the Lord today. Simply ask Him to forgive you and commit your life to Him. Study His Word and live by it and your life will have a peace and joy that you never dreamed possible. A new season awaits you in Christ!

ENDORSEMENTS

Myra has been a treasured friend to me for over 30 years. Over those years, I have observed her walk with the Lord to be consistently marked with diligence and passion for the things of God. Myra's teaching is insightful, inspiring and biblically solid. "As iron sharpens iron" you will find her writing and teaching both challenging as well as encouraging.

Patti Heiselman,
Bethany, Oklahoma

****

Miracles do happen. Myra Woodbridge's life is living proof; she goes from near destitute days to heart stopping adventures in her book. God has given her such creative depth and her journey could have only been planned by God.

Rosemary Nixon,
Atlanta, Georgia

Printed in the United States
115333LV00001B/127-135/P